BY RIVER, STREAM
AND LOCH

BY RIVER, STREAM AND LOCH

Thirty Years with a Trout Rod

A. R. B. HALDANE

Illustrated by Helen Monro Turner

DAVID AND CHARLES: NEWTON ABBOT

0 7153 6101 5

Set in 11 on 13pt Bembo
and printed in Great Britain
by Billing & Sons Limited Guildford and London
for David & Charles (Holdings) Limited
South Devon House Newton Abbot Devon

Contents

Foreword

In the autumn of 1940 I published under the title *By Many Waters* a collection of fishing and other country essays. These were largely accounts of fishing expeditions in which I had taken part in the period between the end of World War I in 1918 and the beginning of World War II in 1939. Since the publication of *By Many Waters* it has been my good fortune to take part in many more fishing expeditions in various parts of the United Kingdom and abroad, and the collection now presented is an account of these further expeditions covering the period up to the present date.

To a large extent, therefore, this new collection may be looked on as a continuation of *By Many Waters*. There is, however, one essential difference between the earlier collection and this one. The former chapters were written all at one time in 1939, in many cases describing events which had taken place many years before. The latter were in the main written contemporaneously, or if not immediately follow-ing the events which they described, at least within a comparatively short time after. I have revised some of the individual chapters to a small extent, but not extensively, feeling that what was written at the time or shortly after was likely to be more accurate in description and to reflect more closely the thoughts and emotions evoked by the scenes and events described than anything written at a later date could do.

By Many Waters and the present collection cover together a period of well over fifty years. My career as a fisherman, however, started about 1905 when as a small boy of five years old I began to fish the streams in the Ochils near my home in Perthshire. The thirteen years between that time and the end of World War I constitute the background of a book entitled *The Path by the Water* which was published in 1944 and which described my early fishing years. These three volumes, therefore, *By Many Waters*, *The Path by the Water* and the present collection cover a fishing career of over sixty-five years.

Few things are more difficult than to convey to others the sense of pleasure enjoyed by writing about it. Many, if they had this gift would, as Lord Grey wrote long ago, 'take the World by storm tomorrow'. In publishing these angling reminiscences I make no claim whatever to the possession of this most rare gift. These latest chapters, together with the earlier ones, have been written largely for my own pleasure in retrospect. I would hope, however, that they may give some pleasure to others, if only in stimulating comparison between their experiences and my own. In addition I would like to think of these pages as being some acknowledgement of the very great happiness which fishing, and particularly trout fishing, has given to me throughout my life.

A. R. B. H.

Foswell
Auchterarder
Perthshire
August 1972

CHAPTER 1

Sea-trout fishing in Connemara

On a sultry evening in the third week of August 1938 I made my way from Buchanan Street station in Glasgow to the Broomielaw. Here on the side of the river, only a few hundred yards from the very heart of the city, one comes unexpectedly on a long row of high sheds marked with the names of some of the delectable places to which Glasgow is the gateway. The first is marked 'Carradale, Loch Ranza and Pirnmill', and from it in the early hours of the morning the steamer *Dalriada* sets off on her journey down Kilbrennan Sound between the rocky shores of Arran and the hazel slopes of the Kintyre Peninsula. The next shed is the home of the steamers which run from the Clyde to the Hebrides, and bears the names of some of the Outer Islands temptingly displayed on its board. But both these I passed and continued down the line until I came to the one marked 'Belfast'; and here my taxi deposited me with my luggage and bundle of fishing rods. These were immediately seized by a burly dock-hand who disappeared with them into the shed while I followed behind, rather uncertainly, for I am not sufficiently familiar with the ways of ships and docks to have overcome the fear of encountering cranes swinging loads of merchandise past my head or of being accosted by officials demanding tickets or passports or some essential document which I have mislaid or do not possess. Inside the shed was great activity. Sacks and wooden crates stood all around, the latter apparently mostly filled with Fyffe's bananas, while several of the dock-hands were engaged in trying to corner a small calf which had got loose and which, when I arrived, was getting distinctly the best of the ensuing chase.

Once on board with my luggage stowed in my small cabin, the first feeling of bewilderment gave way to one of serene detachment and I came on deck feeling at peace with the world and ready to enjoy to the full the spectacle of the loading of the ship and the preparations for sailing. While these were in progress a small party of men who had just come aboard grouped themselves with linked arms near the stern of the ship. I do not know whether or not they were professional singers, or to what extent the emotion under which they clearly laboured may have been the product of previous visits to riverside bars; but for the next half hour, through the creaking of the winches, the shouts of the crew and all the noise and bustle of the ship's loading, came the refrain of Scottish folk songs and Negro spirituals sung with very real if unconscious art and a depth of feeling worthy of the departure of an emigrant ship for a distant land. The last of the cargo to be loaded consisted of a number of motor cars which were quickly and skilfully slung aboard and guided down into the well in the ship's stern watched by the anxious eyes of their owners. I did not see the calf and hoped it had made good its escape from its large pursuers. Then followed the usual ringing of bells from the depth of the ship, and the reflections of the lights of Glasgow on the water were moving past the ship's side as we gathered way. My journey to Connemara had started.

It was quite dark as we slipped down the Clyde, for we had not sailed till 10 pm, but both banks of the river were outlined in a blaze of lights which lit up the shipyards and warehouses as we passed, while the lights from our own portholes reflected on the water below me as I leant over the rail of the upper deck, and on the widening ripples made in the black water by our passing. I could read the names of well-known firms of merchants, of engineers and of shipbuilders on the banks and could feel a thrill of vicarious excitement at the thought of the far places to which the ships of this river go out.

When planning my journey some days before, I had pictured myself staying on deck to see the dark outline of the Arran Hills or perhaps the first signs of dawn over the coast of Wigtownshire, but remembering the long day before me, more prudent counsels prevailed and as the shape of Dumbarton Rock came into view I went below. We made the crossing in a flat calm, and I slept undisturbed till the steward roused me as the ship passed under the shelter of the green and brown hills which stand round Belfast Lough.

In Belfast I met my brother and a friend who had crossed by another route, and later that day we set off in a greatly overloaded car on the first stage of the drive across Ireland. We had been motoring south for a little over an hour when an incident occurred which seemed to us a good introduction to the Irish way of life. A short way ahead of us we saw a small office building with a barrier across the road and men in uniform beside it—clearly the frontier post. Here we stopped and presented our papers to the officer on duty. These he studied with some care and then with growing bewilderment. Presently he approached us and pointed out that our papers had not been stamped on our exit from Northern Ireland. Thinking that we were at the exit point from Northern Ireland we were completely mystified till we learned that we had reached the entry point into Eire having apparently overshot the Northern Ireland post. The stamp of the officer of the latter post being essential for our entry into Eire there was nothing for it but to turn the car and retrace our steps. A short way back we came to another small building beside the road which we had not noticed on our southward journey and where we had apparently not been seen. Once more we presented our papers, this time to the Northern Ireland authorities in the person of the frontier guard. But here a great mystery became apparent. We were now going north, but our papers did not bear the exit stamp of the Eire frontier guards, and without that Northern Ireland could not let us in even for the purpose of immediately signing us out. We were in fact in some sort of official limbo, unacceptable to either State. For a time it seemed that we had posed for the authorities an insoluble problem, with the prospect, for them, of diplomatic complications and, for us, endless delay. I cannot now recall the exact process by which a solution was worked out between the two sets of frontier officials, but good will and humour played, as so often in Ireland, a full part, while our fishing gear was—here as at other times in other lands—held as proof that our intentions were beyond reproach; and so at last we entered Eire duly certified as honest men.

Irish main roads are surprisingly good and as we went south we met with little traffic, but we did not go farther that evening than Mullingar in West Meath where we spent the night. Next day in rainy weather we pushed on west through a flat land of indifferent pasture in need of drainage, alternating with stretches of bog, the fields divided by stone dykes mostly in poor repair. The houses, too, showed signs of poverty. Many of these were cottages with unpointed stone walls, save here and there where stark and ugly new houses had been put up with little apparent attempt at art or originality in their design. Presently there appeared on the horizon a low line of distant blue, which as we went farther west rose and grew into the welcome outline of far mountains. Beyond Galway we entered a bare rocky country of low brown hills. The road, as we went west, grew more and more lonely and the disused railway line to Clifden which it follows added to the feeling of desolation. The permanent way, grass-grown and without rails, the empty station buildings, and the signals standing gaunt and lifeless for ever heralding the approach of some invisible and ghostly train, made it seem as if some dead hand lay stretched out over that desolate moor.

At Carna, on the north side of Galway Bay, which was our destination, a strangely mixed party crowded Mongan's Hotel to the extreme limits of comfort. Some were there for walking and sketching, some to wait for calm weather to cross to the Aran Islands which lie out in the bay just opposite; and there were some, like ourselves, come for the sea-trout fishing. There was a gaunt austere bishop of the Church of Rome who wore purple socks and talked hardly at all, accompanied by his more human and approachable curate-secretary, and there was Mr Cosgrave, then leader of the Opposition Party in the Dail, a kindly if rather unsmiling man to whom one longed to suggest that his holiday would be more restful and comfortable if he wore clothes other than a dark town suit with stiff white collar and cuffs. That this motley gathering was, in dimensions if not also in composition, beyond the expectations of the hotel staff soon became apparent. Despite the absence of what a fisherman calls rain, showers blowing in from the sea and the boggy ground all around combined to produce damp boots and clothes each day. For a time the staff attempted to distinguish the respective owners, but their system, if they had one, soon broke down, and they fell back on the simpler expedient of leaving the guests to select each morning their own from among a pile of assorted boots and shoes, stockings and coats. Perhaps after all the bishop and Mr Cosgrave were happy in their choice of distinctive clothing.

The fishing in the many shallow oddly shaped lochs which lay scattered over the surrounding moorland was fair and we caught quite a number of sea-trout during the next few days. Few of them were over 1lb, the sea-trout of the Irish lochs and rivers being in general, and for some reason which I have never been able to understand, appreciably smaller than those of very many Scottish waters. The burns too were low and fresh fish had not entered the lochs for some time. In the evenings after returning from fishing, we would often set off on foot to explore the surrounding country. This was a land of low rounded hills from which the soil must ages ago have been largely scraped away, perhaps by the action of ice, till the bare rock showed in great sheets and slabs, and only on terraces and in hollows between does soil remain to give a home to the coarse grass, the whin and the brambles which grow luxuriantly wherever they can find a root hold. There seemed little food for the few undersized and athletic looking cattle, and on the hillsides, often far from any habitation, one would come on a donkey standing patient and immovable, its tail to the wind, showing no sign of life but an occasional movement of its long ears. Everywhere were rough tracks, their surface strewn with boulders or blocked with whins so that only the loose drystone dykes enclosing them on either side and the virtual impossibility of passage distinguished them from the more open hillside over which they wandered without apparent goal or object. And over the whole land blew the soft south-west wind from Galway Bay.

One day we explored northward up the lovely road which runs past Lough Inagh and Lough Derryclare and so into that part of Connemara which they call Joyce's Country. Beyond the lochs the road crossed a great stretch of bare moor, bog and rock, a place of utter solitude broken only here and there by an isolated cottage which showed, a little patch of green and white, far out in the surrounding brown. A few miles more brought us down to the narrow winding arm of the sea known as Killary Harbour and to the little group of houses at Leenane near its eastern end; and here a few days later we moved from Carna.

A little way to the south of Killary Harbour lies the group of high hills known as the Twelve Pins, their north slopes draining into the lochs at Kylemore from which the little river Dawros runs down to the sea. It so happened that some of the fishing at Kylemore at that time was unlet and during the few days we stayed at Leenane we were able to fish the lochs and the river, motoring over each morning to Kylemore where Joyce, the old ghillie, met us. The upper loch at Kylemore lies for the most part on bare and open ground where the wind sweeps it from end to end, but the lower one where we fished was a quiet piece of water sheltered among hazel woods. To the north the hillside rose steeply in rocky terraces densely clothed in hazel, rowan and holly. To the south low hazel woods bordered the loch but beyond was open bog-land sweeping down from the hillside above. A small burn coming into view from a corrie far up the hillside fell down the slope in a deep gully. Whether from the dark colour of the brown bog grass and the stunted heather or the steepness of this north-facing slope, the whole of the hollow seemed always to be filled with deep shadow through which the colours showed dark and intense, a shadow which held the eye and challenged it to search more closely the secrets of the gully and the deep corrie hiding the burn's source.

When we reached Kylemore for our first day's fishing, the hazel woods, wet with heavy rain fallen in the night, sparkled in the morning sun, and the lochs had risen to a point which made Joyce doubtful of our prospects. Heavy showers fell at intervals during the day and by midday we were sitting in the boat in pools of water. Among the minor discomforts of life, that of sitting on damp tweed takes a high place, and at lunch-time we determined that we must try to remedy matters. The only available house where we could find a fire was the tiny post-office at the end of the avenue leading to the convent at Kylemore. Here we took refuge, the friendly post-mistress leaving us temporarily in charge of the office, where we dried our trousers and undergarments as best we could before a slow-burning fire, and prayed that none of the inmates of the convent would choose this moment to come in search of postage stamps. Decency was preserved and relative comfort achieved and by the time we left the loch that evening we had, despite Joyce's pessimism, caught eighteen sea-trout, the biggest weighing nearly 3lb. In addition my brother had lost after a long fight a much larger fish, which kept very deep in the water and finally made off in a great rush, at a speed quite beyond the capacity of the reel of the little trout rod to give off line.

On the following two days we again fished the loch, catching altogether about forty sea-trout. Later in the week we tried the Dawros River which by that time had fallen to a good fishing level, and here we got three small salmon besides a few sea-trout. Shortly after it leaves the lower loch, the river widens out into a great pool edged with rushes and weeds save at the neck where an outcrop of rock forms a natural stand for the fisherman. This pool was full of salmon which were continually rolling over and jumping, but though we fished it thoroughly we never found the surface of the pool sufficiently roughened by the wind, a condition, we were told, essential to success. Certainly we found its absence fatal; but great numbers of fish are sometimes killed here and I can imagine that on a good day the fishing of the pool must be a thrilling experience. The rocky slope rises steeply above the point from which the pool is usually fished, so that those not fishing can look from a height which allows the eye to see far down into the water and to watch the fish as they come to the fly. The main objection to this when we were there was that this very spot had been chosen as the site of a very virulent wasp's nest.

Below the rock pool, the Dawros River runs through oak and hazel woods and then out into boggy moorland in which it has made for itself a deep channel. Some of the pools are slow and deep, but in the upper part are many pleasant shallows and runs, while here and there outcrops of rock make short stretches of broken water. One day Joyce took us to the river mouth. It was a lovely morning of sun and wind after showers in the night. As we looked upstream from the old stone bridge which carries the coast road over the rocky mouth of the river, we saw that the spate of the last few days was running off, and the brown and silver of the pools and shallows gleamed and sparkled in the morning sun. The meadows on either side, fresh from the showers of the early morning, were vivid with the green of bog grass and rushes where dark crimson orchis grew, and at the upper end of the green valley were the hazel woods of Kylemore with the high hills of Joyce's Country beyond. Westward, outlined against a sky swept clear by the Atlantic wind, a solitary hill of rock and heather guarded the river mouth looking out to Inishbofin and the open sea.

The local people carry on a line fishing industry of sorts in Killary Harbour, and one day we went in search of a crew who would take us out in their boat. We found the boats drawn far up in a little sandy cove facing out to the islands which lie in the bay beyond the harbour's mouth, and after some difficulty we induced two fishermen to agree to take us. These boats are beautifully built of wood little heavier than plywood, but with a great number of ribs on the inner side to give it strength. The construction is on the carvel principle, with no overlap of the timbers, so that the bottom of the boat presents an absolutely smooth appearance. They are wonderfully light craft, and when the time came to launch the boat, one of the men got his head and shoulders under it and hoisted it, bottom upwards, on his back, walking off with it down to the water's edge looking from a distance as if some great black beetle were marching on its hind legs. The boats are as easily handled in the water as on the land, moving lightly over the heaviest swell, though their lightness and absence of keel make them sensitive to the least touch and difficult to steer. A fresh west wind was blowing, and though the harbour mouth is partly sheltered by the islands of Inishbofin, Inishark and Inishturk, a fair swell was coming into the bay, over which the light boat rode easily and smoothly. We made towards the small islands which lie off the north side of the harbour mouth, trolling meantime for mackerel and the large pollack which abound on that coast. Looking over the low gunwale of the boat, I watched the sand and the rocks on the bottom slowly recede in the deepening water. Seldom have I known such clearness of water. It was as if one gazed through a piece of crystal very faintly tinged with green, so pure and clear that sand and rocks and shells lost to the eye little of their true colour. Only once before had I seen such brilliant colouring in water—on a still night off-shore in the Gulf of Genoa when I lay in the stern of a fisherman's boat watching in the light of an acetylene flare the wonder of the colours in the sea bed.

About midday we landed on the north side of Killary Harbour, the men guiding the boat into a narrow opening in the rocks which made a natural harbour in miniature, sheltered from the wind. Here we bathed and, before dressing, ran along the shore in the teeth of the Atlantic wind. Place and weather combined to produce there in that lonely spot on the extreme western edge of the land a vivid feeling of well-being and freedom.

McKeown's Hotel at Leenane differed from Mongan's at Carna in being on a main through road, so that those who used it were not only people come from a distance on holiday, but included commercial travellers, dealers and farmers moving through the country on their ordinary business. We had our meals at a large communal table in an old-fashioned dining-room with big sideboards on which stood the heavy plated dish covers and massive cruets of the Victorian era. The

B

walls were covered with glass cases filled with stuffed pike and trout from the local lochs and rivers, in number and variety worthy of a museum. The whole, dating from a past age, created a feeling of solidarity and permanence restful and by no means unwelcome. After dinner we would sit for a time smoking on the low wall in front of the hotel, watching the sunset light on the waters of Killary Harbour before going in to sit reading and talking in the upstairs drawing-room till bedtime. Here was a strange mixture of conversation. Dealers and commercial travellers discussed business and prices; a retired colonel from the south of Ireland earnestly advocated the use of the greased line for salmon, while two elderly ladies found their natural setting among the stately Victorian furniture of the room as they exchanged social gossip with a seriousness becoming the importance of the topic.

When the time came for us to leave Connemara, we reluctantly took the road from Leenane back into the hills and so over the watershed to the valley of a little river which runs down to Lough Corrib. As we neared the end of the valley, we came in sight of the blue waters of the loch, its low shores and wooded islands, stretching in the distance, as it seemed, like a great wide inland sea. Yet beautiful as it was, we turned to look back with regret to Joyce's Country, which we were leaving, to the hills which look down on the islands, the bays and the sea-lochs of the west and on the little river mouths where the salmon move in from the Atlantic.

CHAPTER 2

With a trout rod at Monymusk

Easter in 1939 fell in the second week in April. So, by chance or by design, did the climax of the Albanian Crisis. In normal years in peace time, all the good spring salmon fishing in Scotland and most of the good early trout fishing are let much in advance, and only for periods and consequently at rents which put them quite out of the reach of those who can get away from work only for a long weekend, or at most for a few days at Easter. But that year letting arrangements were upset by the Dictators and so it happened that we were able to get fishing for a few days on one of the best parts of the Aberdeen-shire Don.

It was after seven on the evening of the 6th of April when I left my home near Auchterarder by car for Aberdeen, and as I climbed the

hill on the Perth road from the old bridge at Dalreoch, I stopped to
look back on the darkening valley of the Earn where the quiet bends
of the river below me still reflected the last of the evening light. Across
the valley, the fading twilight dimmed the soft folds of the Ochils
sloping up through scattered whin and withered bracken to the bents
and rushes of the tops where curlew and plover had already moved
from the valley to their nesting grounds. In Perth there was delay
for, turning across the Tay eager to be on the Aberdeen road, I overshot a traffic signal and though the police were friendly and sympathe-
tic, it was some time before they had all the details of me and my car
and would let me go on, my eager anticipation of the coming days by
the river but little blunted by the thought of the summons which
might be to come.

Driving alone at night can be a wearisome business, and many times
I have had to draw in to the roadside to sleep off the deadly drowsiness
which so often comes; but that evening it was not so. It was a frosty
starlight spring night; the car was full of fishing rods and landing nets
soon to be in use and, as I drove, impatience and subdued excitement
kept drowsiness at bay. There is great beauty about that road which
runs through some of the most fertile land in Scotland, past parks with
great trees rivalling the best in the English counties and overlooking
miles of rich farmland to the Grampians and the Angus glens. Night
hides this but gives much in its place. It gives the cosy snugness of one's
little world of light, burrowing like a luminous mole through the
enveloping blackness of the arches of surrounding trees, their branches
meeting overhead to make a tunnel of light through the black shapes
on either side; the rich colouring in winter and spring of brown leaf
on beech hedges made more vivid by the light of headlamps. There is
an air of mystery and romance, too, even about one's fellow-travellers
which is at other times absent, and unconsciously the surrounding
blackness links one to them with a sense of fellowship and friendliness
which by day would seem impossible. Of the animals, too, a night
journey by car gives many an unofficial and unaccustomed view.
We sometimes tend, perhaps, to forget how much of the activity
of nearly all the wild creatures takes place in the dark hours. No sight

is more familiar on the roads at night than rabbits and hares taking their ease on this man-made playground. Rats and mice scuttle desperately across from one verge to the other, no doubt thinking of the car as some bigger and noisier species of owl.

As I thought of all this that evening on the Aberdeen road I called to mind how once when crossing the Moor of Rannoch late at night on the old road which went by Inveroran I came suddenly on a hind standing in the road near Loch Tulla. It stayed motionless in the beam of the head-lights till I was within a few yards of it, and then turning towards me charged straight at the car. I could not pull up in time, and a head to head collision seemed inevitable; but at the last moment the hind jumped to one side over the wing of the car smashing one of the head-lamps to pieces as it went. As I got down to inspect the damage to car and beast I could hear the hind moving away, apparently unhurt, over the moor, leaving me in the car to crawl in the light of one lamp to Ballachulish and subsequently to explain the incident as best I could to an indulgent but slightly incredulous insurance company.

To those who have often travelled that Aberdeen road, much that is hidden by the dark comes to the mind's eye. The familiar curve of the road, or the shape of wayside trees, bring to mind the Angus hills to the west, and the lights of Kirriemuir twinkling far over the valley sharpen in the mind's eye the unseen view. Soon the colour of the road surface changes from grey to the pink of the rich land round Laurencekirk, and now the open flat across which the outline of the big hills is barely visible is the part which they call the Howe o' the Mearns. Above the road to the east is rising ground, the highest points covered with clumps of weather-beaten trees, their tops torn and flattened by the gales from the North Sea now close at hand. The road winds down a wooded glen and at its foot is Stonehaven and the coast.

At Stonehaven the character of the country changes. The road skirts the top of high cliffs and here and there is a great cleft in the rocks down which, in the daytime, one can see heaving masses of green water grinding and churning themselves into white foam at the foot of the cliffs. That April night the moon rose over the sea as I climbed the hill out of Stonehaven, and at the top I stopped to watch its reflection on the waves which, far below me and out to sea, looked no more than silver ripples on a pond. A few more miles along the cliff top and the road started again to fall, till a bend brought into view the lights of Aberdeen.

As I crossed the Bridge of Dee, I thought of the day years back when, in the teeth of a strong wind and a flooded river, my seven colleagues and I wearily forced our boat through the bridge in the wake of more youthful and skilful opponents. The occasion was the annual race between the venerable boat club in Edinburgh to which I belonged and the boat club of Aberdeen. Our club, rich in the possession of honourable traditions and ancient customs, suffers the defect of lack of water suitable in width or straightness for the adequate practice of its art. The weed-grown stretches and narrow bridges of the Union Canal immediately to the west of the capital are not well adapted to the needs of the racing craft and at best preclude the use of boats larger than the four-oared type. Perhaps for this reason the activities of the club tended at the time of which I write to be more of the social kind, its rowing confined to occasional four-oared races or more frequent leisurely expeditions by boat to Hermiston a few miles out. Here of a summer evening supper in the lock-keeper's house and a skittle-alley by the tow-path rewarded the painful and unaccustomed efforts of members whose youthful rowing days at the universities were no more than distant memories. A special effort was indeed made each year for the Aberdeen race, but here the limitations of the canal imposed a sad handicap. For the Aberdeen club race in eights, and the best we in Edinburgh could do was to practise in two separate four-oared boats on our canal, hoping that by some happy miracle these could be united on the broad waters of the Dee to form an efficient crew in an eight-oared boat lent by the Aberdeen club for the occasion. Twice four is eight on the black-board, but on the water the resulting sum is less convincing. So it was on the day of which the lights of Aberdeen provoked the memory. The Dee was in flood, while a strong upstream wind raised a violent chop which added to the troubles of our boat, for which a practice row on the morning of the race had not sufficed to unite into one its two parts. Of the race itself my memory is painful. Rocked by the little waves of contending wind and current, and wet from the spray of our own oars a common misfortune did indeed weld us into some sort of unity and for a time we held our own; but soon the enforced lack of practice took its toll of a crew too fresh from the office stools of Queen Street and Charlotte Square and despite all we could do three clear lengths divided our bow from the stern of our opponents' boat before the Bridge of Dee was passed and rest came to us. The race over, our late opponents became our kindly hosts, their further success in the new role to be measured by the less clear recollection of the ensuing hours till our departure later that evening from Aberdeen station.

The night porter of the hotel in Aberdeen greeted me that April night with an intonation which brought a new flood of memories. I saw again the birch and fir woods along the Dee. I heard the porter at Glassel calling the name of the station as the train drew in and knew with a thrill of anticipation that the next stop was my destination at Torphins. I recalled the track winding through broom banks and granite boulders up to the heather of the Hill of Fare, and hot August afternoons when the grouse disturbed by our morning's shooting moved down from the high ground to lie close among the scattered trees and blaeberries at the foot of the hill. I saw in fancy the wide stretch of hill ground across the Dee rising in the west to the massive shoulder of Lochnagar, and to the north the sharp point of Bennachie standing, an eastern outpost and a sentinel to the hills by Don and Deveron.

My room in the hotel overlooked the station, and that night I lay awake listening to the rumble of the wheels and the puffing and shunting of engines in the sidings. There is something friendly and comforting in the sound of trains at night; not so much in the quick busy express but rather in the humble goods train pulling slowly out as if knowing that it has far to go and must be content with a leisurely pace. I see in fancy the cosy red glow from the engine cabin and the light from the van where the guard keeps his lonely vigil through the night. I see the train tucked away out of the path of the express into the quiet security of some moorland siding. Before I slept, a goods train drew out of the shunting yard. I lay listening to the trundle and clank of its trucks till they died away in the distance on the line to the north. I pictured its leisurely journey through the green flats of Buchan, or turning westwards to follow the windings of the Don and so over the high ground to Strathbogie and the Deveron. Perhaps it would cross the hills to the valley of the Spey, or take the line north to the coast where the morning sun would find it dawdling along between the fishing villages of the Moray Firth; and so, with my thoughts a-wander in green and quiet places, I drifted into sleep.

In the morning my brother joined me after the arrival of the London train and we breakfasted together discussing the news and the prospects of being able to enjoy a peaceful weekend on the river. The news from the south was not reassuring, but the Aberdeen morning paper told us that the Prime Minister had left for Donside so it seemed that all must be well. At least our hopes were shared by those in high places. After breakfast, we took the road to Kemnay in the clean brightness of that April morning, moving through air so cold that the glittering points of light reflected from the crystals of pink and grey granite on the roadside walls might have been particles of frost catching the morning sun. Young grass was showing in the lee of the plantations and by the burns and springs; plover were calling over the plough and curlew on the hillsides as we followed the road towards the distant snow-capped top of Bennachie. Before midday we were at Kemnay and, leaving our luggage at the hotel to be unpacked in the evening, we set off with rods, nets and waders to find the keeper who was to show us the limits of our water. Apart from ourselves, the upper Monymusk beats had no tenants that week so that we had several miles of unknown water to fish. Salmon were running and we had learned that the trout were rising during the midday hatch of flies. Signs of spring were all around; in the olive-coloured catkins hanging from the hazels and in the birches whose bursting buds showed tiny specks of green among the dark tracery of the twigs; in the fresh green of dog mercury and anemone under the trees; in the flight of oyster-catcher, sand-piper and wagtail along the banks and over the shallows.

There is endless and fascinating variety in each day's fishing; in the play of light and shade on pool and stream, on tree and hill; in the friendly nearness of animals and the tameness of birds; in the hatch of fly and the rise of trout, and in all the infinite changes and chances of fortune. These few days at Monymusk were among the pleasantest of any I remember since first I fished. They were days of spring sunshine beside perfect trout water with hatches of fly towards midday worthy of Test or Itchen and short fierce rises of trout while the hatch lasted. With so much excellent water and so little time at our disposal the problem was to decide where to fish. Good as it all was, one was often tantalised by the thought that other parts yet untried might be still better, and indeed it often happened that the hatch of fly was thick on one pool and relatively meagre on the next. So from first to last we covered some miles of water and only towards the end of our few days did we learn to concentrate on the pools and streams which we gradually came to single out as the best among such wealth. The trout were of all sizes, but those we got—fifteen or twenty of them each day—averaged nearly ¾lb, with a few larger. There were spring salmon in the water, too, but they would not rise readily to fly; and though, inspired by the success of a man on the opposite bank, the ghillie who came out with us now and then tried hard to induce us to fish for them with minnow, we had little inclination for this and if the trout were not rising, preferred to idle on the bank and watch his own unsuccessful efforts.

I sometimes fear I shall never be a persevering or very successful salmon fisher, perhaps because I have seldom fished in first-rate salmon water at the best of the season. The presence of salmon in the small sea-trout rivers of the West Coast adds wonderfully to the thrill of expectation, and more than one day has, for me, been made memorable by a fight with a salmon on a trout rod. But to labour all day with a heavy rod on broad water is to me at times something of a penance, tempered only by the multitude of little things which make up so much of the charm of fishing. At such times I find it a relief to hand the rod now and then to the ghillie if one is at hand and to sit resting by the waterside letting the drowsiness which comes beside dappled and eddying water 'slide into the soul', or to take a light rod and try for trout in the shallows and along the edges of the streams. At Monymusk one could do this with little sense of wasted or lost opportunity. For the mill-dykes of the lower Don impede though they do not prevent the upward passage of the salmon, while the richness of the valley and the quality of the soil provide in river-bed and waterside conditions under which the natural food of the trout thrives and multiplies. So it comes about that the Don is still at least as good a trout stream as it is a salmon river.

From the wood which they call Paradise up to above Tillyfoure on the Monymusk water was a succession of lovely streams, pools and shallows, and to see them during a hatch of fly and a rise of trout was an object lesson in the rich prodigality of nature. The water seemed alive with trout of all sizes and even the salmon took a hand, though whether the fish we sometimes saw making head and tail rises like huge trout, were fresh fish or kelts, I could not be sure. At Tillyfoure the daffodils were in bloom, covering the grassy bank which slopes to the edge of the river. I coveted that bank and pictured warm evenings in late June when one could be fishing within a moment of leaving the house with no long tramp in waders to blunt the sharpness of anticipation or the joy of retrospect.

In a long broad pool immediately above the daffodil bank of Tillyfoure the trout one morning rose in scores. The deeper part of the pool near the tail was out of the reach of our trout rods, but on the edge of the broken water near the neck we could reach the rising fish, and this part, while the fly lasted, we found most productive. Towards midday the main hatch of fly began to fail, but a few big flies, of the mayfly type, started to appear, and far out in the broken water at least one salmon broke the surface, tempting us to casts beyond the capacity of our rods. Tired at last of an occupation fruitless of result and costly in tail flies, I went off upstream to explore a broken stretch of water some way above. As I picked my way among the boulders and rough ground of the water's edge I watched the stream for rises. In the swift broken water there were few signs of trout till I came in sight of a place where a cluster of large stones near midstream threw the main current towards the far bank. In the few yards of sheltered water in the lee of the stones trout were feeding rapidly and greedily. Flies were in the air rising and falling near the pool's surface and others were drifting round in the eddies behind the boulders, but none came within reach of me where I stood on the bank nor came near enough to show me what kind they were. For these were flies hatching from the gravel of the river-bed, some to be eaten by the trout before they reached the surface, others to meet the same fate as they dried their new-found wings on the top of the water and only a few to enjoy a short life in the April air, to mate and in dying to give the chance of precarious life to a future generation on a spring day of another year.

Despairing of being able to identify and imitate the fly on the water, I made the best of it with a large hackle March Brown which I had used in the stream below, floating it again and again across the little pool, down the edge of the fast current on its far side, or letting it drift round in the back-water nearer to me. These were big trout. Some seemed to be fish of 1½lb or more, and it was maddening to see them take, as they constantly did, natural flies floating side by side with my own which they ignored; but every now and then one, tired of uniform diet, would take my fly, though none but the smaller ones did so till at last a really big one swallowed my March Brown only to rush straight out into the strong current where he broke the cast. All at once the flies ceased to hatch, the rises stopped, and I found myself watching a seemingly lifeless pool as I added yet another to my memories of missed opportunities and lost trout.

On the afternoon of our second day, I had gone upstream to where the Monymusk water on one bank faces that belonging to Castle Forbes. As I came down to the river with the intention of fishing a stream for trout, I found myself nearly opposite an elderly gentleman fishing for salmon in a deep stretch just below. Not wishing to interfere with the salmon fisherman I sat down some way back from the river to watch him. He fished with a heavy rod, and great energy, putting into each cast an almost vicious cut as if knowing already that his fishing was soon to be interrupted by unwelcome tidings. In days to come historians may well find scope for fruitful research into the influence of sport on the course of political and military events. The history of our country from the time of Drake onwards would, I believe, provide many examples. Certainly in the second decade of this century the story of British foreign policy leads the reader to the banks of the Findhorn, the Cassley, and constantly to the Itchen. So the history books of the future may record how much of chance and how much of careful planning went to the timing of the events in Albania in April 1939.

When Mr Chamberlain (for he it was) and his ghillie had left the pool I moved down opposite to where he had been fishing and stood looking across to the far bank, partly, I think, just out of idle curiosity. It looked an unpromising piece of water, deep and slow and feature-less, but as I watched, a salmon or a very large trout made a leisurely rise in the centre of the river. I cast my trout flies over him, and he came at me at once. The rise had not looked like that of a spring sal-mon and the first few minutes as he bored heavily down into the deep water convinced me that he was a kelt, and a kelt he proved to be; but even a kelt on a trout rod can be exciting. As an old Tweed fisher-man once said of kelts, 'Aye they're a nuisance, but, man, they gie ye a fine hurrl' – and the next few minutes were not without pleasure. For all that, my enjoyment was tinged with some anxiety lest Mr Chamberlain and his ghillie might return upstream. The pool, and the fish—such as it was—were rightly mine, but I could not help imagining what my own feelings would be were I burdened with the responsi-bility for the fortunes of my country in a crisis which even then seemed to threaten its very existence, and if on top of it all during a blank day's salmon fishing I found a total stranger playing what would seem at first sight to be a spring salmon on a trout rod in a pool which I had just fished. The fisherman may well feel doubt as to which affliction would be the harder to bear.

In his fishing diary Mr Chamberlain describes this day on the Castle Forbes water:

> I decided that I would wait till today when H. J. Wilson was to ring me up after a meeting of Ministers before deciding whether to come back by 'plane or train. I stayed about and packed and

did a box [of despatches] during the morning and after hearing Horace W. decided that A and I would take the evening train from Aberdeen.

In the meantime I went out for a last try. Fished the Nursery from the far side, saw 3 fish and got a pluck from one. Then to Upper Deepstone where I had a good pull from the 2nd point. Afterwards went to Lower Deepstone where touched nothing (saw 1) and back to Island Pool where failed to rise a fish that Humphreys had seen. Crossed the bridge and fished Nursery and Mid Deepstone without result. This was the end.

The political anxieties were too overwhelming to allow me to get any satisfaction out of this 'holiday'. I was conscious of want of concentration and bad fishing.

In the late afternoons when the wind came cold up the valley from the North Sea, we would make for home. After dinner we would drowse over our books by the fire and later before we slept would walk a little way down a side road to a quiet stretch of the river, where standing on a bridge we looked over intervening fir woods to the peak of Bennachie, sharp and black against the north-western sky. On the Sunday before we left Donside we climbed to its top, wading through deep heather and young planting on the lower slopes. It was a day of thick easterly mist blowing in from the sea when we started, but this began to clear away as we neared the top and then the sun broke through to give us a view far up the valley to Alford and Strathdon and the tangle of hills in which the river rises. To the east the ground fell gradually to green rolling lowlands changing to blue distance and then to silver-grey haze over the coast. Later we climbed down a little way on the north side of the hill, and finding a sheltered grassy ledge below the summit we sat to eat our lunch, our backs against a sloping rock and our faces warmed by the spring sun. Far below was a wide expanse of heather and peat bog where cock grouse were calling, while nesting curlew soared and glided filling the place with the joy of their sound. After a time, a cold wind made us move as the sun lost its strength and the mist crept up again from the sea;

but not before we had soaked ourselves in the warmth and peace of that hillside, our eyes and perceptions perhaps sharpened by the knowledge that the time for the quiet enjoyment of such things was already running short and that we must store up the memory of them against a time to come.

CHAPTER 3

Spring-time on the upper Don

The mellowing light of a May evening filled the broad valley of Strathmore. Rich red plough-land stood out in vivid contrast to the green of spring grass and fields of young corn dotted with nesting plover and the brown hunched shapes of feeding hares. On the east side of the valley cattle, feeding on the low hills behind Laurencekirk, moved slowly to the upper edges of their grazing, following the sunlight as it receded before the growing shadow thrown by the hills of Glenesk across the Howe o' the Mearns. Twilight had almost come when we reached Aberdeen, and as we walked by the harbour in the late evening the riding lights of ships moored to the quayside shone across still water. Peremptory notices and barbed wire fences to keep unwelcome visitors from certain parts of the docks brought to mind recollections of our last visit to Aberdeen in 1939. Then, as now, we were bound for Donside, but oppressed by the shadow already growing over Europe—a shadow which, deepening into night, was now, in the late spring of 1945, almost past.

There is a wonderful freshness about the Aberdeenshire countryside in spring-time, and as next morning we left the city behind us and took the Deeside road, I felt a lightening and an exhilaration which in the last six years had seemed an unattainable and almost forgotten experience. Memories of other journeys up Deeside came flooding back. With them came the assurance that those things the loss of which had seemed so probable to us on Bennachie in 1939 had after all been preserved and that the capacity to feel and enjoy them had not been spoiled by the intervening years.

For a few miles up the Dee the greyness of a sea mist persisted, but as we went west we came out into the bright cold of a May morning. A fresh east wind drove high clouds in from the North Sea. By the roadside wild life, intent on its own affairs, seemed little disturbed by our passing, and in one field a pair of partridges hardly looked up from their feeding close beside the roadside hedge. Plover and sand-pipers called over the pasture fields and the broom banks, while oyster-catchers and an occasional tern marked the nearness of the river, the silver glint of which came now and then through the birches.

Beyond Banchory, the windings of the road alternately opened and hid the view up the valley of the Dee to a rim of high hills in the west. At Dinnet we left the valley of the Dee and took the road which climbs northwards through birch and pine woods to the upland farms of Logie Coldstone, and on to the heather and scattered trees of the watershed. Soon the land was falling to the north into the valley of the Deskry Water, and in a few miles we reached the main road up Strathdon and turned westward beside the river.

Our first sight of the Don on that May morning was something of a disappointment. We had last fished the river at Monymusk many miles downstream, and while we were prepared for a much smaller river, it seemed impossible that trout of any great size could be got in what seemed in places little more than a large hill stream. Rain earlier in the week had put fresh water in the river, but this was now running off. The stream looked shallow and stony, lacking the deep pools and the quiet water of the stretches below Alford; but we had been assured that large trout were to be got, and that early in the season as it was, a few salmon had already made their way up to these top waters. Our first few days were to change our view of the upper Don, and on closer acquaintance we were to find that surprisingly large fish were to be caught even in quite shallow water, while there were deeper pools, some capable of holding salmon, where really heavy trout might be caught.

The upper Don rises quickly after rain in the hills, but falls correspondingly fast, and with the glass now rising and small prospect of further rain in the near future, it was of importance to us to be able to fish at the first opportunity. In view of this it was unfortunate that our first full day at Strathdon should, like many another good fishing day, be 'snappit up by the Sabbath'. These were the days of strict petrol rationing, but careful economy during the weeks immediately preceding our holiday and the fact that our small car was not a thirsty one, had left us with enough petrol for a very little running in addition to our journey to and from Donside. So on that first Sunday morning we took the road up the valley, past the dark pool below the bridge at Poldhulie, past Inverernan, through the little hamlet of Corgarff and on to Cockbridge. Here the river, shrunk to the size of a hill burn, continues upstream into the hills to its source in the high ground which divides the Don basin from the Avon. At Cockbridge we crossed the stream, and climbing steeply on the north side followed the Lecht road which, in the troubled times which followed the Rising of 1745, the Hanoverian government made over the hills to Morayshire.

After climbing from the Don Valley, the Lecht road follows for a few miles a ridge of high and heathery ground. At the point where the road starts to fall on the north side, we left the car and climbed westward up a shoulder of rising ground on the very borders of Aberdeenshire and Banffshire. Boggy ground and peat hags, showing no sign of life except the mournful calling of a pair of golden plover, nearly turned us back before we had gone far, but climbing on we came at last to hard bare ground closely covered with crisp grey lichen on which our feet crunched as if on icy snow. On top of the shoulder we ate our lunch, looking north-west to where the Avon Valley leads down to Morayshire. The cloud drift was from the south-east and the distant

C

view was softened and dimmed by the grey haze, which a southerly wind so often brings. To the east, the rounded bulk of the Buck of Cabrach loomed through the haze, and to the west we could dimly see the east face of Ben Macdhui and snow patches on the rounded ridge of Ben-a-Bourd. Southward the top of Lochnagar rose above the high ground dividing Don from Dee. There was little wind and no movement on this high shoulder, and only the faint sound of distant running water came up to us as we lay in the lichen.

On our way back to Strathdon we stopped at the top of the hill above Cockbridge and looked across to where the old barracks of Corgarff stood below us, stark and deserted, their lonely setting unrelieved and rather intensified by a nearby clump of leafless weather-beaten ash trees. Before we took the Donside road, we went a little way up the side road which leads to Delnadamph and stopped the car at a point where we could get a near view of the barracks. Surrounded by bare uplands, with high walls and small windows staring out, now blind and lifeless, into the hills, they stood gloomy and austere, but in the foreground sheep grazed and lambs played in a green field, where oyster-catchers hurried to and fro in the pasture.

In the week that followed, the last of the flood water ran quickly off; but the moisture stored up by the melting of the winter snows kept the hill springs full, and while the river fell to a lower level it remained fishable though very clear. The water which we were to fish starts about three miles above Strathdon, extending upstream to where the stone bridge at Luib crosses the Don a mile below Cockbridge. Each morning the hotel car started up the valley, dropping off successively at the top of each beat the rod to whom that beat had by rotation been allotted. Shortly after 10 am on the morning of the 23rd of May the car dropped me a little way below the hamlet of Corgarff, my beat extending downstream for rather over a mile. The southerly wind which had limited our view from above Cockbridge on Sunday had changed into the north-east and blew upstream, cold and bleak, and for a time there was little or no sign of flies or fish; but by 11 o'clock the sun came out and with it a few flies started to hatch. For the first hour I fished downstream using small wet flies. This first hour produced little, but the few rises which came, mostly in the rapid necks of the pools, showed that the stream did indeed hold much larger trout than had seemed possible. As the day grew warmer a few trout started to rise to natural flies and as the wind blew steadily upstream the reel was changed for one with a greased line and the cast for a tapered one with a small medium olive. Towards midday, olives started to hatch in considerable numbers and with trout now rising freely to them I concentrated entirely on the dry fly method, regretting the fact that I was at the top rather than the bottom of my beat.

The main rise lasted from midday till 2.30 pm and during these hours the hatch of fly would have borne comparison with that to be seen on any of the English chalk streams. The upstream wind made it necessary to walk round each pool to the lower end giving it a wide berth, sometimes wading through broom banks, the rod held high overhead, or clambering over the drystone dykes which in the hill districts of Aberdeenshire are often eked out with makeshift additions of barbed wire, sheep netting, wooden rails and bed-ends, efficient perhaps for deterring wandering stock, but less admirable for the fisherman. As I turned upstream at the tail of each pool the water during this midday rise seemed alive with trout, feeding with slow head and tail rises, with noisy splashes and often with little leaps clear of the water on the olives now rising from the surface or blowing off the banks and shingly beaches.

In the early afternoon I came to a deep narrow pool where the Don takes a sudden turn beneath a rock face overhung with hazel. The current flowed fast along the rock face, but on the nearside was quieter water of some depth. Wading in below the tail of the pool and moving slowly upstream to within casting distance, I saw two good trout rising against the rock face near the tail, but looking past them up into the deep quiet water there seemed to be the movement of a much larger fish deep down against the brown stones of the bottom. I had almost decided to try first this upper part of the pool, risking the disturbance of the trout below when one of the latter rose again, a rise so tempting and at such an easy distance and angle that I floated a fly over it. The fly was immediately taken. A trout of $\frac{3}{4}$lb in a narrow rapid stream and

hooked on a small fly at the end of fine gut is not easily controlled, and
before he could be stopped he had reached the deep quiet water above
and had jumped. The small pool being now hopelessly disturbed I gave
up hope of getting anything more from it and waded up to the quiet
water to land my trout on a shingly beach near the neck of the pool.
As he came in to the net, I looked down into five feet of water where a
salmon cruised round and round, rudely and completely disturbed. For
a moment my ¾lb trout, fat and firm and lovely though he was, seemed
to shrink to miserable proportions till I reflected that almost surely a
salmon confined in such a pool and in such low water would hardly
have looked twice at a small olive.

Leaving the rocky pool I turned again downstream. Immediately
below, shallow rapid water stretched for some distance, and going a
little way I sat down beside a broomy bank to eat an overdue lunch. At
my back, yellow-hammers called from the wooden rails of a fence at
the edge of the broom, and beyond in a little haugh ewes were grazing
while lambs ran races in the young grass among heaps of fresh damp
earth thrown up by moles stirred to activity by the spring weather. At
my feet the shallow stream of the Don rippled over stones edged here
and there with clumps of kingcups growing to the water side. Speedwell and wild pansies, yellow and purple, covered the banks, and under
the willows across the river wood anemones were still in bloom, for in
this meadow 1,000 feet above the sea the flowers of spring had over-
lapped with those of early summer. Opposite to where I sat, birches on
the steep hillside flecked with the green of the young leaf were alive
with nesting chaffinches and tits.

A little way downstream a fold in the hillside opposite filled with
heather and juniper led upwards to the higher slopes and farther still to
the skyline where scattered trees stood out against the blue. If I had to
choose one characteristic which more than another seems to mark the
valleys of the Dee and upper Don I would choose the woodlands. In
many parts of Scotland the greatest altitude at which forest trees will
flourish is not much more than 1,000 or 1,500 feet, but in parts of
Aberdeenshire, and most noticeably perhaps in the valley of the Don,
that upper limit extends to 2,000 feet or more. So it is that here, one

walking beside the river sees above him great woods of larch and pine stretching in places to the rounded tops of the surrounding hills. The wastage of two wars has done much to thin these woods on Don and Deeside, but much remains, and where areas of wood have been cut, nature has quickly clothed the naked hillside with thick carpets of blaeberry plants, apple green in spring, coral-coloured and crimson in autumn. Even the gaunt survivors of wholesale timber-cutting add vividness and wildness to the scene. On parts of the unplanted ground, natural seeding of the trees has taken place, and scattered through the heather on the lower slopes of the hills are pines and larch trees in ones and twos and little groups whose isolation has saved them to flourish and grow old in untutored and natural beauty.

These wooded slopes above the Don brought to my mind as I sat by the river Professor Gilbert Murray's translation of the words of Phaedra the Queen in the *Hippolytus* of Euripides as she lay weak and ill and longing in her fevered mind for the freedom and freshness of the hills:

> Oh, take me to the mountain, oh,
> Past the great pines and through the wood
> Up where the lean hounds softly go . . .

Perhaps she remembered some Aegean slope where, as on the hills of Donside, the woods climb up and up, thinning as the higher slopes are reached, till on the topmost ridge the trees stand gaunt and weather-beaten against winds blowing in from the sea.

After a time my eyes and attention turned from the distant woods and the horizon to the river at my feet where flies were still hatching and blowing upstream, pursued now and then by a pair of pied wag-tails whose home seemed to be a gravel bank edged with willow across the river. The best of the rise was past, but a few trout were still feeding as I fished on slowly through the afternoon, catching one more trout big enough to keep and returning several to the water. The lower end of the beat was marked by a small farm and a sawmill, and here late in the afternoon I came, tired and contented. Crossing the last meadow through the smell of new-sawn wood I came out on the roadside, and

sat down to wait for the car, resting legs and hands and eyes, and counting the seven trout of $\frac{1}{2}$lb or over which had been kept out of the
fifteen caught since morning.

Two days later I again fished the upper river, this time on the top
beat. The car dropped me at the stone bridge at Luib where the road
crosses the Don before climbing the ridge which overlooks Corgarff
barracks and Cockbridge. It was a fine morning with high cirrus clouds
overhead and the promise of real warmth later in the day, clearly a day
for a dry fly. As I stood on the bridge to put up my rod, a few flies were
already blowing upstream under the arch and before the cast was on, a
trout in the deep pool above the bridge had started to feed. For a little
time I leant on the parapet of the bridge enjoying the quietness and
beauty of that cup in the hills and relishing to the full the knowledge of
the long day to come. Then as the morning grew warmer and the hatch
of flies thicker, I tied on my faithful friend the olive and started off
downstream. A fish rising under willow bushes on the far bank near
the bridge proved unassailable, but a little way below, trout were rising
in a short deep pool where a big boulder lay in midstream near the tail.
Rusty wire from some old fence washed downstream showed at one
point above the surface. The feeding trout were fortunately rising in
such a position as to give a chance of fishing for the lower ones without
disturbing those above. Casting a dry fly from well below I was able
to hook the lowest fish and, helped by the force of the water, to pull it
quickly downstream and land it—a fish of 10oz and a good beginning
to the day. The next was feeding well above the boulder in the middle
of the pool and it, too, allowed itself to be pulled down without
disturbing the water above; but this was a larger trout and once out of
the pool it ran on downstream in shallow rapid water where I had
little control over it. Seeing my predicament, a crofter mending a fence
nearby came to help, and despite the well-meant efforts of his collie
which raced along the bank barking, he was able with my long-handled
net to land it in a tiny corner of quiet water some distance below. This
fish weighed 1lb, and though not in such good condition as the first,
was a highly satisfactory addition to the basket. The third trout in the
pool by the boulder was rising well up in the neck. It was clearly the

best of the three, and when it took my fly confidently it seemed that the Fates were indeed being kind; but this fish had grown in cunning as in size. Knowing well the possibilities of the submerged wire the trout made straight for it, and before it could be stopped had doubled round the wire and broken the cast, much to the annoyance of the crofter who had stayed to watch my efforts and whose disappointment was as great as my own.

There was no more to be done in that pool, so tying on another fly and leaving a trout with the crofter, I walked on downstream. All through the morning trout rose freely to a steady hatch of flies. About midday I came to a narrow foot bridge, the old planks, bleached silver grey by sun and rain, covered with olives in all stages of their short lives. Below was a long shallow stretch and as the trout now showed signs of becoming gorged and fastidious, I sat down leaning against a steep heather bank to eat my lunch. Opposite to where I sat, the hillside rose gradually to a far sky-line and half way up the slope there ran through the heather the clearly marked track of an old road, leading downstream to disappear at a bend a mile below. This was the track of the old military road from Corgarff barracks to Gairnshiel and Deeside, and as I looked it needed small effort to picture files of red-coated soldiers moving through the heather, making for Corgarff on one of the weekly patrols which in the years following the Jacobite Risings alone linked the English garrisons at Corgarff, Tarland, Inchrory and a dozen other remote outposts isolated in a wild and hostile country. But the track was older still, and long before the English soldiers came it must have known the tread of weary cattle, stolen from the pasture lands of Strathardle or the Angus Glens; for this was one of the routes by which the old cattle reivers drove their stolen beasts to their strongholds in Badenoch or Lochaber. The main purpose of the garrisons established after 1745 in the hill country between Don and Dee and Spey was to stop this lawless traffic, and after 1750 when Scotland at last emerged into an era of peace and prosperity, the road knew again the tread of cattle as the drovers took their beasts south to the trysts of the Lowlands.

The old track had led my thoughts far away in time and space, but now I turned again to the river and in a little while moved on downstream. Soon I came to a point where the Don turns sharply back towards the Strathdon road. At the bend were a number of good pools from one of which another trout of 1lb was added to the basket after a hard struggle. This nearly ended in disaster, for the fish ran beneath a wooden foot-bridge and for an anxious moment the line was caught on one of the upright supports as with difficulty I followed to net the trout on a gravel bed below. Beyond the bridge a stretch of shallow water with no clearly marked pools appeared to offer small prospect of fish and I had started to walk downstream, paying only casual attention to the water when the sudden appearance of several good trout darting out from under the near bank, disturbed by my passing, showed that the water called for more care. Making a detour through rough grass and rushes, I came again to the bank some way below. Looking up-stream, few rises were visible, but it seemed worth while floating the fly at random over what appeared to be the least shallow part of the water in midstream. This plan proved very successful, and two more good trout were added to the basket, besides a smaller one which had to be returned. The experience reminded me of the lesson learned before, but often forgotten, that on the Don and the Deveron at least, good fish may be found in quite shallow water. One of these trout taught me another useful lesson. The fly had floated over what seemed the most promising piece of water and was indeed already below me as I knelt on the bank; but the fly was floating so well that I let it float on to the end of the slack line available. At the very limit of the line, and several yards below me, a trout rose and was hooked. As I played it, I made a resolve to remember in future that when fishing the dry fly in rivers such as the Don or the Deveron so long as the fly continues to float without a drag it is wise to leave it on the water and not to assume that every fish immediately downstream has of necessity been disturbed.

By now my time was running short and the last quarter of a mile of the beat had to be hurried over to enable me to keep tryst with the car near Corgarff church. As we ran down the valley on the way home, I looked with gratitude and no little wonder at the stream which, so far up in the hills and within only a few miles of its source, had on this perfect spring day produced a basket of nine trout whose average weight was little short of ¾lb.

On the evening of our last day on Donside, we walked a short way up the side road which follows the south bank of the river. Beyond the little church at Strathdon the road climbs steeply past hanging woods of beech and larch which look down to the brown gleam of pools and the silver glitter of shallows as the Don winds below. Opposite Canda-craig we turned off the road through a thin wood of old larch trees and came out on a slope where blaeberries grew round the stumps of pines cut a few seasons earlier. Looking up the valley we could trace in the failing light the bends of the river from the pasture fields at our feet up through the narrowing glen to the distant hills above Corgarff, dark against the evening sky. Beyond the open ground on which we stood stretched uncut woods climbing the shoulder of the hill. Farther still they climbed, till, outlined against the sky, the farthest trees stood scattered along the ridge where at evening mountain hares and deer would emerge from the sheltering woods to watch from their safe retreat the valley and the river far below.

CHAPTER 4

On river and loch in Wester Ross

A hundred miles to the north of the point where the River Awe bursts through the Pass of Brander to carry the waters of Loch Awe on their short, impetuous course to Loch Etive, Nature has set on a rather smaller scale a scene of like character. Here on the coast of Wester Ross-shire the waters gathered from the mountains to the north-east of Loch Torridon, from the high ground around Kinlochewe and from the south face of Slioch move slowly westward past the wooded shores and islands of Loch Maree before entering the short River Ewe which carries them to Loch Ewe and the Atlantic. The little village of Poolewe lies at the head of Loch Ewe overlooking the narrow rocky mouth of the river. At high tide the salt water fills the river's mouth, quietening the meeting of river and sea, but when the tide goes out it leaves a rocky barrier over which the river falls to the loch in a tumbling mass of white and brown under the stone bridge on the Ullapool road. Here, in September 1948, we came in search of the big sea-trout and salmon which make their way up the River Ewe into Loch Maree and finally to their breeding grounds in the streams which feed the loch.

The late summer of 1948 had been, in many parts of the country, a time of almost unprecedented rainfall. The early autumn was little better, and as we came down the road which leads north across the ridge from Gairloch we got our first sight of a river, the size and speed of which raised unwelcome doubts as to the adequacy of our rods and tackle. It was as well for our peace of mind that we could not foresee that the gales of the autumn equinox were that year to come before their time and that wind and torrential rain were to sweep the coast of Ross-shire for the next two weeks.

The sea-trout and salmon fishing at Poolewe consisted at that time of rights of fishing the river on certain days in the week, besides limited rights on three beats at the extreme westerly end of Loch Maree. In the latter days of June and during July and early August when the greater part of the big sea-trout and grilse run, the best of the fishing is in the lower part of the river, but by September many of the fish have passed up into the loch or are tending to congregate in the upper reaches of the short river. At its extreme west end, Loch Maree narrows suddenly between the shoulder of Ben Airidh Charr on the north side and the rocky face of Creag Mhor to the south. Closer and closer come the shores till soon the loch is little more than a narrow lagoon running between woods of birch, oak and hazel. For the first few hundred yards the narrow waters, sheltered by the surrounding hills and woods, are smooth and placid and only here and there do slight eddies or the trailing of the weeds below the surface tell that the current is already flowing rapidly. A little farther and the draw of the stream grows stronger. The shores close in still more, and now the stream running deep, but with great strength, passes through a narrow channel about forty yards across. These are the upper narrows of the River Ewe. Once more the shores recede and the stream eddies and boils as it merges into the quieter waters of a narrow loch between the trees. Again the shores close in to form a second narrow channel with stone jetties on either side, the middle narrows, through which the river passes with increasing speed. Below this the

river again broadens out into a second small loch of great depth at
the far end of which the water passes through the lower narrows
to enter at last on the mile of rapid stream which ends in the salt water
of Loch Ewe.

In the two weeks of September 1948 when we fished at Poolewe,
the lower pools of the river were at a level which made them, if not
unfishable, at least very far from their best fishing condition and our
hopes and interest were centred mainly on the narrows. Hope ran high.
A steep heathery bank overlooks the middle narrows on the north
side, and sitting here on the Sunday immediately fo lowing our arrival
at Poolewe we watched with growing excitement and impatience
the big fish which rolled and jumped in the smooth glide of the stream
in numbers which exceeded our most sanguine expectations.

The river beats on the Ewe and the beats on Loch Maree fished
from Pool House Hotel were at that time allotted on a basis of rotation,
those recently arrived at the hotel taking their place at the foot of a
rota through which, as the days passed, they gradually ascended. It
was a system as fair and as fairly administered as could be wished for,
but one which added yet another hazard to the uncertainties of fishing. Our arrival at Poolewe happily coincided with the departure of
several fishermen. So it was that our initial place in the queue was
more exalted than might have been expected and during our time
there three days on the narrows fell to our lot. The first of these began
unfortunately. The middle narrows are fished from both sides of the
river. Our ghillie advised us to start from the left bank which entailed
crossing by boat the small loch into which the middle narrows widen.
Before we crossed, it seemed worth while putting a fly over the lower
narrows near which the boat was moored. The smooth glide of the
swift stream slightly ruffled by the morning breeze invited the use of
the greased line and a small Blue Charm tied on a light hook. As
the fly floated round in the smooth water immediately above the
first break of the rapids it was taken by a heavy fish which made off
downstream. The 14 foot rod and cast of medium weight offered at
least a fair chance of turning it, but after a moment of strain the line
came back. To lose a heavy fish at the very outset was bad enough,

but disappointment turned to anger when it was found that the iron of the hook had broken at the bend. As the years pass the fisherman grows to some degree reconciled, or at least hardened, to many types of disaster which he recognises as his common and inescapable lot; but a hook broken by the mere weight of a heavy fish in strong water may well seem to him an affliction which he might reasonably hope to avoid. So at least it seemed to us on that September morning.

All through that first day fish showed themselves at frequent intervals and in considerable numbers in the middle narrows. Some were of the type which leap far out of the water and appear to stand on their tails indicating all too clearly to the fisherman that they have little interest in him or his activities; some barely broke the surface with head and back like great trout feeding, raising hope and expectation to the highest pitch; but the morning breeze had died away leaving a surface of glassy smoothness in which even the smallest of salmon flies was ignored and a blank day was redeemed only by one small sea-trout which took an olive dry fly thrown upstream with a light trout rod.

Our second day on the narrows a few days later was more successful. An upstream breeze rippled the surface of the middle narrows and a salmon of 13lb taking a small Silver Grey was soon landed, while a second fish moved twice at the same fly but failed to take hold. Our third day on the narrows was more productive and far more exciting. This was in our second week at Poolewe and in the meantime heavy rain had raised the river to a great height. Knowing that the fish were moving more and more towards the upper reaches of the river and into Loch Maree, our ghillie advised us to concentrate on the upper narrows, though these, at the height the river had now reached, could only be fished from a boat, and that with difficulty. It was a fortunate suggestion. It so happened that the small boat which lies in the narrow water at the extreme end of the loch was not in use that day. Pushing out in it, our ghillie allowed the stream to drift the boat down towards the upper narrows while we sat in the stern ready with the salmon rod. As we neared the narrows the pace of the current increased and only by hard rowing against it could the boat's progress be slowed sufficiently to allow time to fish the water. Gusts of gale force blowing directly up the river drove in our faces drenching showers of rain and spray. To our eyes focussed on the rapid stream it seemed that the rocks and trees of the shore were all in motion, while the swinging of the light boat and the force of wind and rain produced a lively and thrilling sense of battling with the elements. The boat had drifted through the narrowest part of the channel out of the strongest of the current when in the rough choppy water caused by the meeting of wind and current a salmon rose to the fly but missed it. Turning the boat into a backwater out of the main current the boatman again forced her a little way upstream to drift a second time over the same area. In almost the same place a fish rose again. This time there was no miss and soon we were playing a heavy salmon in the swirling eddies of the widening river where we had been swept many yards below where the fish had been hooked. The slacker water helped the rod and it was not long before the fish allowed itself to be led into a backwater near the north bank where we landed for the final and successful struggle with a salmon of 21½lb. The small double hooked Blue Doctor seemed little the worse and soon we were battling against the current as the ghillie again forced the boat upstream. This time he held the boat as best he could in the main stream while the fly was cast into the quieter water at its edge near the south bank. Here a fish took with a fierce rush hurling itself half out of the water as it seized the fly with unusual savageness. There could be little doubt that the fish was securely hooked and the fight which followed was largely a repetition of that which had just taken place but characterised by short fierce rushes much in keeping with the peculiar rise to the fly. The stronger play of the fish suggested a salmon of greater weight than its predecessor and it was with some surprise that as the struggle neared its end we got glimpses of a fish appreciably smaller. Not till it came in finally to the gaff and turned on its side did we see the large spots of a trout and guessed that this was one of the very large sea-trout for which the Ewe and Loch Maree are famous. To put the matter beyond doubt some scales were later sent to the Fishery Board in Edinburgh where they were confirmed as being those of a cock sea-trout in its thirteenth year. The reading of the scales showed that the fish had spawned no less than nine times and was now on its tenth return to fresh-water. The scale-readings of salmon show, I believe, that it is rare for a cock salmon to survive more than one or at the most two spawning journeys, and the fact that a cock sea-trout can survive a similar adventure so many times raises one of the many problems of fish life to which an answer has yet to be found. The fish weighed just short of 15lb, and on our return to Edinburgh we drank to the memory of an exciting day from the bottle of excellent sherry at that time offered by a firm of London wine-merchants to those fortunate enough to catch a sea-trout over 8lb.

The capture of the two big fish and the repeated passage of the boat might well have disturbed the pool, but the upper narrows must that day have been alive with fish, for pushing out in the boat again we were soon fast in a third one; but this time over-confidence proved our undoing. The fish was far from exhausted when we made a premature landing on the north shore. Running far out into the strong current it went off downstream so fast that the line, sticky near the backing from long neglect, would not come off the reel fast enough and after a painful moment of tension the cast broke.

The light was now beginning to fail and the blasts of icy rain had become almost continuous. So we went home in a happy but somewhat chastened mood trying to think of the two fish caught and not of the third of at least equal size lost through what I well knew to be my own unpardonable fault. The loss of that last fish was, however, a well-disguised blessing, for never since then have I failed to dry my line after use, and what was initially a nuisance has now, I hope, become a habit. I am aware that the makers of certain of the many floating lines which have come into such common use since these words were written claim that it is unnecessary to dry them after use. Nonetheless, since 1948 I have made a point of running off both trout and salmon lines, whether floating or non-floating, each evening after use.

One day early in our second week at Poolewe we fished one of the beats at the end of Loch Maree. Those who fish that loch regularly are, I understand, divided into two main categories. There are those, perhaps the majority, who use the method common on the Irish lakes, known as 'dapping' and who regard it, with some reason, as the best and most effective method of catching the big sea-trout in the loch. Others, while recognising the effectiveness of dapping regard it as a somewhat passive method of fishing calling for little of the finer art and skill of wet fly or orthodox dry fly fishing. In support of their view they claim that in dapping the comparative novice may be little less successful than the skilled fisherman, though I understand that the hooking of a fish rising to the dap is by no mean easy. I have no intention of entering the lists on one side or the other having, in any event, insufficient experience of dapping to make my views of any value. I would only say that for my own part, from the very little dapping I have done, I think it probable that I shall continue to prefer to fish a loch with wet or dry fly.

That first day we fished on Loch Maree was a day of moderate easterly wind falling at times almost to complete calm, and our basket was light. When the breeze was at its strongest we tried dapping, having with us a reel with floss silk line, but the breeze was not sufficiently strong or steady. Wet fly was more effective and with it we got one or two fish, but only one of any size. The largest we got that day—a sea-trout of between 2 and 3lb—rose to a small Greenwell's Glory fished as a dry fly. Numbers of big fish were constantly showing themselves, however, and as the west end of the loch was evidently full of them we decided a few days later to try fishing late in the evening after a day on the hill lochs.

An old road leads down to Tollie Bay at the extreme south-west corner of Loch Maree, and here a few evenings later we came to try for sea-trout in the failing light. Above the stone jetty where the boat is moored, the side of Creag Mhor goes steeply up, the lower slope clothed in hazel and covered with a gigantic tumbled mass of moss-covered boulders of every shape and size. The midges were terrible, and it called for some strength of mind to thread the line and tie the knots in the face of almost intolerable itch and irritation; but once we were afloat the midges left us in peace, presumably to turn their attention to whatever occupies the time of the midge in the long bleak tracts of its life when no human is available to bite or annoy. The breeze had fallen with the twilight, and now as the light failed only the faintest ripple came down the loch from the east. The calm evening seemed to call for dry fly so I had a greased line and a 2X cast on the $9\frac{1}{2}$ foot rod while my companions preferred wet fly. My fly was an Iron Blue—the very largest in my box. I never remember the numbers of the different sizes but it was about $\frac{1}{2}$ inch long. The oiled fly floated well on the calm water, and watching that smooth surface, black and sinister in the heavy shade of the hillside, one could not but feel a thrill almost of fear for the fate of that small thing tempting the monsters moving among the jagged boulders far down in the deep loch. My hopes—or were they fears!—were justified for, as I watched, a black head and shoulders, seeming immense in the dim light, broke the surface and engulfed the fly. After a wild rush outwards the fish turned and came with equal speed towards the boat, ending the rush with a jump along the surface towards the boat almost as if intending to attack us. The line, which in desperation I had pulled in by hand, lay coiled anyhow at my feet and for several long seconds that fish was complete and undisputed master of the situation. When after an anxious interval the slack line was reeled in and once more tight it refused to run through the rings of the rod. In the confusion of the moment the slack line had taken a turn round the end ring of the rod top, and it was only by great good fortune that the fish remained quiescent while the rod top was hastily lowered to my companion at the far end of the boat who put matters to rights. From now on the chances were fairly even, for the cast though light was new, the water was deep and free from weed. The fish, after its first display of originality, fought in a stubborn but orthodox way and at the end of a quarter of an hour we gaffed a sea-trout of 7lb.

By now the light was so far gone that it was impossible to see a dry fly on the water, but we added two more sea-trout, one of over 2lb, to the basket with wet fly before turning for home. Into the jet black shadows of Creag Mhor the boat moved through the calm water. Here and there a big fish still jumped far out in the loch, but for the

D

rest all was still. Dew lay on the grass and on the mossy boulders beside the stone jetty as we landed, and across the loch the clouds had drifted down to hide the crest and the upper slopes of Ben Airidh Charr. The midges had gone to bed and beneath the hazels only a few moths fluttered in the lights of the car as we followed the old track to the Gairloch road.

Those fishermen—and there must be very many—who have read with pleasure Osgood Mackenzie's book *A Hundred Years in the Highlands* will recall in particular the chapter which describes the wonderful trout fishing on Fionn Loch during the second half of last century. Now it is only fair to say that, as the author points out, the majority, though by no means all, of these huge trout were caught by trolling, which perhaps detracts not a little from the claims of Fionn Loch to be regarded as being among the great trout-fishing lochs of Scotland. Nonetheless, the record of fish caught at that time is a remarkable one. At the time of which I write (1948), large trout were still being caught on Fionn Loch, mostly on the troll, though not in anything like the numbers recorded by Osgood Mackenzie. At the time of our visit to Poolewe it was possible to hire a boat on Fionn Loch if one were prepared to face the long steep road which was then in a very rough state for a car. We were anxious at least to see the loch and, though we were not equipped for trolling, to take our chance with the trout. So a few days after our adventure at Tollie Bay we set off up the hill road with our excellent old ghillie Mackenzie.

After the rain and the wind of so much of the past week the weather had changed as suddenly and completely as it can on the North-west Coast, and from a clear sky a warm sun shone on a landscape where the lochs lay blue among hills and woods now turning from green to golden brown. There was no wind and as we came down to the loch side we saw that unless a breeze came later in the day our chances of trout were very small. All through the forenoon we fished the bays which lie to the south of the inlet where the boats are moored, taking advantage of any little scraps of breeze which came, counting ourselves lucky to catch a few quite small trout, but seeing nothing of the monsters which we knew lived there. At lunch time we landed at the head of a large bay and sat among the heather looking far over the loch. Presently a few large flies started to hatch and were blown out from the shore. At first nothing stirred on the loch except now and then a very small trout; but presently we saw what we had hoped to see. Far out from the shore, a hundred yards or more, very large fish started to move at long intervals and far apart. At first they were so far out that we could only tell that they were very large, but presently one trout rose rather nearer and we could see that it might well have figured in Osgood Mackenzie's records. These trout were rising at such long intervals, both in time and distance, that it seemed quite hopeless to fish for them, but they were evidently so big that after a time we launched the boat, at least to get nearer to them and perhaps in the faint hope that one might rise within casting distance. One indeed did rise about thirty yards from us, but thirty yards is an impossible distance to cast with a trout rod, and in water so calm it would have been folly to attempt to move the boat hurriedly. It soon became obvious that the chances of hooking one of these fish were almost negligible so, while keeping our lines and flies ready for instant action we settled down to watch for the rises. In this calm water the eye was at once caught by even a slight break in the surface, and so though the rises were relatively few and far between it was possible to study them with some care. After watching a few we came to the conclusion that these big fish were moving very slowly just below the surface which they broke now and then with great deliberation. A typical rise seemed to be the emergence of a small part of the head or shoulder followed at an appreciable interval by the tip of the tail. One fish we saw appeared to lie almost stationary as its head and then its tail broke the surface. I was reminded of the behaviour of basking sharks which we had watched one warm calm day in the channel between Skye and the island of Scalpay. What size these fish were we could only guess. Osgood Mackenzie records several of well over 12lb in his list of catches in 1851, and watching these fish on this September day of 1948 it seemed that several of them might well be in the same class. Presently a breeze came down the loch from the south-east and on the roughened surface it was no longer possible to see a rising trout at any distance; but the experience had been a thrilling one and had shown to us that the Fionn Loch still holds monsters as of old.

The hills which look down on Poolewe and Loch Maree have, as the years passed, seen many changes. Centuries ago when the shores of Loch Maree were clothed in forest the north side of the loch was the scene of one of the very earliest attempts at iron smelting in Scotland. Early in the seventeenth century iron smelting on a more serious scale was carried on near Letterewe. The remains of an iron works, perhaps an off-shoot of the Letterewe enterprise, can still be traced on the right bank of the river a short way below the lower narrows. This was locally known as the Red Smiddy, and the stone cruives still in existence are believed to have been built to supply water-power to work the hammers. Traces of charcoal burning have been found along the shores of the narrows, and it seems probable that the deep streams among the trees which today know only the occasional passage of small boats and the sweep of salmon lines once knew the passing of larger craft loaded with charcoal or the floating of timber from the shores of Loch Maree. Examination of the waste material found at the site of the Red Smiddy shows that the ore used was partly of local origin, but that ore shipped to Loch Ewe from Lancashire or the south of Scotland was also used. A century later Poolewe was the centre of shipping traffic from Lewis and Harris and till well on in the nineteenth century a substantial traffic in black cattle entered Loch Ewe, the beasts and their drovers following the old tracks on the north side of Loch Maree or by Gruinard and Braemore to the trysts of Ross-shire and Central Scotland.

Another century passed, and twice within the space of thirty years Loch Ewe was again a scene of great activity. During the First World War it served as an anchorage for the Home Fleet in the days before Scapa Flow was established as the main base. Again from 1939 to 1945 the Navy used it extensively, and here and there on the shores of the loch and on the rocky headlands which look out to the Minch can still be seen the remains of emplacements for the guns which guarded the Fleet and the merchant ships which gathered in Loch Ewe for the convoys to Russia.

As we left Poolewe on our return to the south we stopped where the road leaves the river, and looked upstream towards Loch Maree. The river was still in flood and a great stream was sweeping down through the old stone cruives and past the site of the ancient smelting works. Beyond, in the calmer waters of the narrows, we could see the occasional splash of salmon as, heedless of the changes in the works of man, they passed from sea to river and loch and at last to the far head-waters, playing their part in an endless and unchanging cycle.

CHAPTER 5

Winterberg in Westphalia

Some years before the war the German State Railways published a fascinating map of Germany for the information of British travellers visiting the country to fish. All the larger and many of the smaller rivers are shown, and over the whole of Germany are marked in red the initial letters of the German names for the principal species of fish to be found in each area. Over the whole of the great North German Plain stretching from Emden through Hanover and Berlin to the River Oder and the old Polish frontier the letters 'H', 'B' and 'Z' predominate, for the lakes and slow deep rivers of this great area are the homes of the pike (*Hecht*), the bream (*Blei*) and the perch (*Zander*). Farther to the south a broad belt on the map stretching from Cologne eastwards by Weimar and Dresden to Breslau and the headwaters of the Oder is dotted at frequent intervals with the letter 'F' for this is the land of trout (*Forelle*). Southward again lies an area which the map shows as shared between the pike and bream of the River Main and the trout in many of its tributaries, but southward once more trout are predominant in the streams of the Black Forest which drain to the Neckar and in many of the tributaries of the upper Danube.

In the early summer of 1952 an opportunity occurred for my wife and me to visit Germany. Our intention had been to hire a car locally as I had done when fishing in the Black Forest in 1934, but currency restrictions made this impossible and it was only through the kindness of relatives serving with the British Army of the Rhine that we were able to carry out that part of our plan which was concerned with the trout of South Germany.

About a hundred miles to the south-west of Hanover lies the small town of Winterberg. It lies almost at the highest point of an area of rolling wooded hills from which run many small streams, some northwards to the head waters of the Weser and some south to the Rhine. It is an area closely dotted on the fishing map with the letter 'F', and for Winterberg on the 11th of June we set out from our base near Hanover, taking with us our trout rods and tackle which had already accompanied us, unused, to the Austrian Alps. At Bielefeld on the main line to Cologne we left the train and entered the bus which was to take us south into the hill country. Seating accommodation, on a very ample scale, was provided for twenty-five people and the springs of the vehicle had clearly been designed accordingly, with the result that for the next four and a half hours my wife and I, in common with our one fellow passenger, experienced the sensations of small peas rattling in a very large pod. Across the flat Westphalian Plain we rattled and bumped at high speed and in considerable discomfort over roads lined with ash and walnut trees, and many acacias, their creamy blossom already withering and falling; but after passing the town of Paderborn we entered the upland country, and as we followed the road winding steadily up to the higher ground, the beauty of our surroundings made us forget the minor discomforts of the journey.

Here was a country of rolling hills and narrow valleys where little rapid streams edged with mint and mimulus ran through meadows deep with summer flowers; a land of many small villages and groups of farm buildings, where against white and cream-washed plaster showed the black timbers of wall and gable. The high steep roofs overhung the walls with deep eaves where nesting martins flew in and out in the sunshine, and in the gardens the cherry trees were laden with fruit already ripening to yellow and black. The sides of the small valleys were covered with a mosaic of little squares and strips of barley and rye and root crops, for here, as over much of Germany the land is intensively cultivated in small farms worked by peasant farmers and their families. The farm work during these post-war days was done largely by manual labour and we saw few implements more modern than an occasional horse-drawn cultivator clearing the weeds between the rows of the root crops. Far more often this work was being done by hand by the women of the farm, and time and again we passed little patches of roots where the whole family on hands and knees were laboriously weeding the crop or singling the plants. On the hillsides cornflowers showed through the bright green of the half-grown barley and round the edges of the tall patches of blue-green rye growing on slopes which looked down on meadows where the flower-filled hay stood ready for the reaper. So in the late afternoon of the June day we came at last to the upland plateau where Winterberg stands on open meadow ground looking out over fold upon fold of gently undulating wooded hills drained by the streams which we had come to fish.

The position of Winterberg at the source of a number of streams flowing some to the north and some to the south is a commanding one offering for the fisherman an admirable variety of experience and opportunity, but in June 1952 the problem of transport was gravely complicated by the slender nature of our resources. Within a short distance of the town the streams which have their sources in the upland springs around it have grown to a size sufficient to house plenty of small trout, but to reach a point where deeper pools and heavier fish were to be found meant a drive of ten to fifteen miles. Anxious calculation, however, led us to the conclusion that on our first day at least we could pay for transport without mortgaging too seriously our future mobility, so after breakfast we set off in a car down the valley of the small River Lenne which rises near Winterberg and flows south to the Rhine.

During the drive to Winterberg on the previous day we had been charmed but rather puzzled to see small children in ones and twos and little groups wading in the tall grass of the roadside and in the upland meadows gathering into baskets the heads but, it seemed, only the heads, of marguerite and campion and other meadow flowers. Now as we passed through the little villages along the headwaters of the Lenne the reason for the flower-gathering of yesterday became plain. For this was Corpus Christi Day, and all the villages were flower bedecked for the great yearly festival of the Catholic Church. Presently we came to the outskirts of the village of Lenne beside the growing stream. A way-side shrine was filled with white flowers and a path of flowers led up from the road to the Crucifix. Now we saw why the children had been gathering only the heads of the meadow flowers, for along the centre of the road ahead of us stretched a carpet about four feet wide of flowers and evergreen. At either side of the strip a broad edging of pale green spruce shoots bordered a solid carpet of blossom. Here in the centre of the carpet the heads of marguerite, scabious, cranesbill and red clover, of broom, white lilac, cornflower and campion were laid in many different patterns of white and yellow, red, mauve and blue while at either side of the road stood lines of young green birch branches. Even the sawdust from the mills beside the stream had been used, and dyed in red and blue and yellow, it had here and there been laid in squares and crosses and diamond shapes to play its part in the weaving of the lovely carpet. Following slowly down the narrow strip of open road between the flowers and the branches of the roadside we came through gathering crowds of villagers to the centre of the village, and past the church to the door of which the flower carpet led.

Our driver left us at the bridge at the far end of the village promising to come for us again at 6 o'clock. Here immediately below the village the main body of the stream ran in a deep lade to drive a sawmill at the lower end of the next meadow. Having decided to walk to the mill before starting to fish we were about to set off down the road when round the nearby corner came a slow procession. First came the village musicians playing solemn church music followed by a group of little girls in white some with nosegays and some carrying small baskets of flowers. Then followed the young men forming the main body of the procession, some carrying banners and crucifixes and in their midst under a canopy walked the priest in all his vestments

attended by acolytes swinging incense. Last of all came the old men of
the village. As the musicians stopped playing the entire procession
took up the music, singing slowly to the rhythm of their marching.
The whole effect was one of great solemnity, and as we stood by the
roadside to see them pass we could not but feel deeply impressed by
the reverence which found expression in this solemn ceremony dating,
as we later learned, from the time of Pope Urban IV in the thirteenth
century, and by the thought of the hours of work and devoted care
which had been given to gathering the flowers and laying the lovely
carpet—the traditional tribute to a Conqueror.

Crossing the roadside fence at the sawmill we walked down to reach
the river bank where the water from the mill rejoined the main stream
at the head of a small deep pool. As we stood in the meadow to put
up our rods trout were rising at the small flies which danced close
above the surface of the stream. Dark green dragon-flies of vivid but
unfamiliar appearance flew up and down the banks and presently a
large butterfly passed down the bank with a swift birdlike flight. It
lighted on the leaf of a nearby alder bush to spread its wings, and
going carefully up to it we realised with a thrill that we were having
our first and almost certainly our only view of a Camberwell Beauty.
The main part of the wing was a rich brown velvet, but each wing
was edged with a border of cream, a line of tiny blue spots
appearing between the brown and the cream.

The pool by the mill stream was much overhung with willow and
alder, but considerable care and manoeuvring for position was rewarded by a rainbow trout of ¾lb which took a wet fly in the rapid
water and fought as only a rainbow trout can. Long and sometimes
bitter experience has taught me to mistrust too early success in a day's
fishing and for some time after this we achieved little except enjoyment
of our surroundings. The main body of the stream ran opposite to us
under a steep wooded hillside from which overhanging trees bending
their branches to the water formed a strong defence for the trout
which rose beneath them. One of our rods was equipped with a dry
fly, for by now a few duns were floating on the water, and now and
then a may-fly appeared, though we never saw anything approaching

a real hatch of the fly. Perhaps because of the relative scarcity of fly these German trout ignored the rules of the game scrupulously adhered to by the trout of the Itchen and the Test, and instead of feeding continuously in one spot or over a very small area, they cruised at will beneath the trees, a habit which gave to them an unfair advantage and to us an undue amount of unrewarded exertion. But despite our immediate lack of further success we were well content. The morning sun shone down on the valley with growing warmth. Along the river bank we waded through beds of mint and yellow flag; behind us the meadows stood deep in campion and buttercup, cranesbill and marigold, and beyond the meadows we looked to a wooded hillside beneath which stood scattered peasants' cottages and farm steadings, their old timber beams black against the colour-wash of their walls.

After a time we came to a little weir where to our annoyance a large part of the stream was again led off in a deep lade towards a corn mill some way below us. The diminished main stream was too small for successful fishing so we walked down the lade to start again below the mill. Here our fortunes changed, perhaps because instead of starting off by catching a good trout I started off by stepping on an insecure stone in crossing the stream and falling headlong into shallow water. Here below the mill, meadows bordered the stream on either side. Willow trees and alders still lined its bank but there were fewer overhanging trees and casting was easier. The river bed too was narrower and the stream deeper, with smooth swift stretches where the water flowed over clean gravel and trailing weeds, between beds of water buttercup. The growing warmth of the day too was in our favour. More fish seemed to be on the move, though most of those we caught were under the arbitrary size-limit of $\frac{1}{2}$lb, which we had set for ourselves, and a few proved to be grayling. A late lunch followed by a long rest on the bank in the hot sun cut far into the afternoon and presently, finding that much of the stream was again led off to feed a mill, we turned once more upstream towards Lenne and our rendezvous with the car. Passing the corn mill we walked slowly up the side of the lade as it ran swift and quiet, deep-set between beds of tall flags and reeds. The breeze blew up the lade and we were tempted to

float a dry fly here and there at a venture on its smooth surface.
A mallard and her brood splashed out from the reeds but turned downstream leaving undisturbed a fish rising a little way above—a fat trout
of about ½lb which we added to the bag. At the sawmill where we had
started in the morning we took down the rods for the last short walk
along the main road to Lenne where by the bridge the car was waiting.

The flower carpet on the road was crushed and dusty from the day's
traffic as we took once more the way through the village and up the
valley. It seemed a shame that such a lovely thing should be so soon
spoiled, but the withered flowers had played their full part in the
festival of the Church, just as the growing flowers of the meadows
had added so much to the pleasure of our riverside day.

Looking back on the day we had spent by the Lenne we were greatly
tempted to return there next day despite the budgetary crisis which
threatened us; but that evening a fellow-fisherman in the hotel, the
happy possessor of a car, offered to take us to try another of the many
rivers within reach of Winterberg—a larger river reputed to hold
heavier trout. We were anxious in our short time to see as much as possible of the surrounding country and its streams, so, promising ourselves that some other year we would revisit the Lenne, we gratefully
accepted our friend's offer and next morning we made an early start
for the River Diemel which flows northward from the Winterberg
hills to the Weser. The map shows that the Diemel rises within quite
a short distance of Winterberg, but the part which we were going to
fish lay well downstream involving a journey of over thirty miles.
Our friend had unfortunately to be back in Winterberg in
the early afternoon and as this would involve leaving the river
immediately after lunch, the long run to the fishing was a distinct
drawback; but indeed we would have been hard to please had we
seriously grudged that journey through lovely wooded uplands and
down little valleys where the morning breeze was shaking the blossoms in the meadows and making little waves of green and silver
through the patches of barley and of rye.

A stone bridge crossed the stream near where the water from a mill
lade rejoined the main river, and here we ran the car into a side

track and put up the rods. In size and character the Diemel reminded me greatly of the Gloucestershire Coln at Fairford. It seemed to be at least double the size of the Lenne and promised easier fishing; but we found it in fact just as difficult, for the banks on either side were much overhung with willows, while in the bed of the river it-self the stream was constantly obstructed and split into small channels by patches of weed and water buttercup. As at the Lenne a few flies were hatching all through the morning and a very few mayfly, but there was no big hatch of fly, and the trout which were feeding were clearly having to work for their living. Many rose under the trailing branches of the willows where they were always hard and often im-possible to reach.

With banks deep in grass, and reeds and trees and bushes growing completely wild and unpruned, some parts of the stream were quite unfishable, more particularly since we had been unable to include in our luggage for Germany anything in the nature of waders; but these drawbacks were compensated for by the quietness and seclusion of the valley and the knowledge that here we were fishing under conditions as natural as could be desired.

All too soon our watches told us that time was running short and we turned upstream again, fishing only rapidly and at intervals on our way back to the car. Even the few hours' experience of the river seemed to have made a difference, and now on the way back it seemed easier to succeed where before we had failed. By the time we regained the bridge we had caught rather over a dozen trout, but of these only two, of 10oz and 1lb had been kept, besides a grayling of about 2lb.

On our way from Winterberg in the morning we had followed down the valley of a small but attractive looking stream before leav-ing it to turn northward at the small town of Olsberg. Now on the return journey our friend offered to leave us near Olsberg to fish up the stream, sending the car for us later in the evening. The stream proved to be full of trout, but their size was disappointing. Fishing rapidly upstream we came to a dividing of the waters. The right-hand branch seemed on the whole the more attractive but after going only a short distance we were hailed by a German farmer. His dialect was broad and my knowledge of German is slight, but his tone of voice and gestures left little doubt in our minds that he claimed the fishing as his private property. By now we were tired and disinclined to argue the point, so returning to the junction of the streams we took the left-hand branch and coming in a short distance upon a bank deep with blaeberry plants on the shady side of the valley we climbed to a little hollow and sat down to eat the last fragments of our lunch, to smoke and to revive our rather jaded spirits. For long we lay there shaded from the heat of the day. Below us the stream ran through fresh green meadows. Across the valley the hillside climbed to thick woods of fir which clothed its upper slopes and stretched to the sky-line. Somewhere above us we could hear the cry of buzzards and presently we saw them—two specks against the blue—soaring on motionless outspread wings far up above the wooded horizon.

The heat of the afternoon passed, and after a time we left the shady bank and waded again through the deep uncut meadows to the edge of the stream. For a short distance at this point it ran in a narrow rocky bed. The current was swift but the pools were of some depth, and narrow as the stream was, there was in places room to float a dry fly on the surface. In this way we got a few trout, but though fat and vigorous none were quite $\frac{1}{2}$lb and we returned them all to the water. In the meadow above, the stream broadened out. In this thin and shallow water we had little hope of getting any but very small trout, and with our time now running short we left the stream and sat on a grassy bank at the roadside waiting to intercept the car on its way to meet us at Olsberg. From where we sat we could trace the stream as it meandered through the meadows, its twisting course marked by the willows and alders growing along its banks.

The road back to Winterberg followed the dwindling stream and led us past farm steadings and through small villages to the head of the valley. Before it climbed to the final ridge the road passed through a stretch of meadow land, a little fold in the hills, surrounded by woods, where a patch of flags and rushes among the flowers marked where a spring came from the hillside—the very source of the stream which we had been fishing. As we looked at the birth-place of the River

Ruhr—for such it was—we pictured the steel-works, the collieries, the factories and the great towns nourished and sustained by this same river in its maturity 50 miles away, contrasting the beauties of Nature with the grim and sordid works of Man.

CHAPTER 6

A trout stream in the Black Forest

More than twenty years had passed since I had last fished in the Black Forest when, on an evening in the first week of May 1956, my wife and I stepped from the train at the little town of Wildbad. We had come by air, flying first to the busy airport of Brussels, and then to the quiet of Luxemburg where larks rose from the spring grass beside the runway at the airfield and hawks hovered in the distance. Then on again over the upland meadows and wooded hills of the Moselle, across the Rhine to Stuttgart. Here by the narrowest of margins we caught the connection to the main line junction at Pforzheim where we changed into the small local train which climbs the wooded valley of the River Enz to the terminus of the line at Wildbad.

Signs of the war were still plainly to be seen in Stuttgart, along the valley of the Neckar and in Pforzheim, but these were soon left behind as we entered the hills. The forest, the meadows and the valley with its riverside sawmills were as I had seen them in those far-off days before the war, and in Wildbad itself as we followed the porter up the narrow

König Karl Strasse clutching our precious bundle of fishing rods and looking for trout in the quiet stretch of the river beside the street, it seemed that little had changed. As we turned in to the Hotel Post off the market place, the door was opened by the old porter, a little greyer, a little slower in the step, but the same Adolf Kromer who had first greeted me there in 1934.

When planning this latest visit—my fourth—to Wildbad, I had been at some pains to find out how the Wildbad trout had come through the war; but in this I had met with small success. All I had been able to learn was vague in the extreme. The fishing, I was told, had suffered from the war, but by re-stocking it was hoped to restore it to what it had been, and it became evident, as I might well have known, that the only way to learn the facts was for us to go ourselves and fish. One useful thing only had I learned: that a state permit as well as a local permit was now required, and that the former must be obtained by personal application at Calw, a small town about fifteen miles north of Wildbad. We had arrived at Wildbad on Friday and as the Calw office closed at midday on Saturday, it seemed that only by catching a bus at 6.30 am was it possible to get the permit before the weekend. Adolf, the porter, to whom trade union hours and restrictive practices of all kinds were unknown, called us at 5.45 am, and as the church clock in the square chimed the quarter past the hour, we set off for the station where the Calw bus starts.

The road to Calw leaves the valley of the Enz at the village of Calmbach, a mile below Wildbad, and after following the smaller valley of the Little Enz for a short distance climbs from it into the forest. Perhaps the contrast with the hot and tiresome journey of the day before had made our minds and our eyes more than usually receptive to the freshness of this lovely May morning, for that drive to Calw lingers in the memory as one of rare beauty. In the village gardens at Calmbach the cherry trees were white with blossom, the apple orchards pink with the bursting buds. The clear water of the Little Enz sparkled below us as we climbed the hillside. In the forest the silver-grey stems of the tall firs and the russet brown of the pines rose straight from a carpet of deep moss and blaeberry, and there was no brezee to stir them. There had

E

been frost in the night, and as we came over the watershed to the high north-facing meadows, the grass sparkled in the first of the morning sun. The small streams ran clear and brimming full, and along their banks and beside the little pools were kingcups in single flowers, in clumps and in golden masses.

Calw is a little town set in the narrow valley of the River Nagold, a stream at this point slower flowing and rather larger than the Enz. The town rises steeply above the river. Cobbled streets, alleys and narrow stone stairways wind between cottage gardens and little orchards up to the woodcutters' roads in the forest above. It was 7.30 and shops and offices had not yet opened. We crossed the quiet market place and came at last by a cobbled alley and many stone steps to a narrow road which overlooked the town and led upwards to the woods; and here we rested. It was very quiet. From the steep brown roofs of the tiled and wood-shingled houses far below, blue smoke rose straight to drift slowly in the cold stillness of the morning. The air was clear and sparkling, but far up the valley of the Nagold the distant wooded slopes were softened by a faint blue haze foretelling the heat of a brilliant day to come. Across the road, violets and a scatter of wood anemones grew on the steep side of the hill under the yellow catkins of hazel and the pale green of the young birch. Slowly the town below us came to life. Housewives threw open upper windows to hang their bedding to air in the morning sun, and forest workers came up the steep road on their way to the woods. The church clocks below us chimed, and presently we climbed back down the stone steps and so to the market place where women were making their early purchases of fruit and vegetables from stalls set out along the pavements.

Our halting German was rusty from long disuse, but *Forelle* (trout) is a magic word in Württemberg and opens many doors. For all that, the issue of our permits occupied the undivided attention of an eager and friendly official and his typist-secretary for the best part of an hour, and when in addition we sought for information about the Nagold and its tributaries, the willing but quite useless efforts of other members of the staff who were called in to consultation must have made appreciable inroads on their morning's work. At Hirsau, a nearby village to which we later walked, the Burgomaster's son, President of the local Angling Club, gave us what little help he could and then we passed the time till our bus left, dozing on a grassy terrace beside a woodland road.

Back at Wildbad, the Town Hall equipped us with a local permit. This was a formidable document; a narrow strip of white cardboard $1\frac{1}{2}$ feet long with a map of the river showing the parts we could and could not fish and peremptory regulations printed in three languages. Armed with this and the product of the Calw officials we felt that at least the authorities had done all they could, and that now the future lay with us.

The town of Wildbad owns fishing rights over nearly ten miles of the river, the town itself lying approximately midway between the upper and lower boundaries. Before the war, I had found the lower section much the more productive. Here the trout were appreciably larger than in the section above, and in the wider, slower-flowing water the fishing was not unlike that of an English chalk stream. Memories of this part of the water filled my mind, and on the day following our trip to Calw we took the train to Calmbach, the village below Wildbad. The day was perfect. The meadows were green with young grass sprinkled over with the white lace of cow parsley and dotted with the mauve of lady's smock which we also call milk-maid or cuckoo-flower. Kingcups and forget-me-nots filled the ditches, and as the heat of the day grew, flies came out in quantities and floated on the surface of the river. Only the rings of rising trout were needed to complete the happiness of the fisherman; but of trout there were no signs. Dry fly, floated over the most likely looking pools, and wet fly were alike of no avail and hourly our forebodings grew. Passers-by whose lack of fishing knowledge was as obvious as their desire to be helpful, wearied us with talk in rapid German, only the general drift of which we could follow. Some blamed the French in whose zone of occupation Wildbad lay; some the unusual floods of the past winter. We remained sad but unconvinced. It seemed impossible that, short of wholesale and persistent poisoning, the occupation forces could have left a completely depopulated river, and to talk of the effect of great winter floods seemed nonsense. Nonetheless, the facts seemed beyond question. The feeling grew that the answer to the mystery lay in something more sinister and less transient than war conditions, and when that evening we made our way back to Wildbad, we were hot, tired and much depressed.

The Wildbad authorities have wisely decreed that there shall be no fishing in the river where it flows through the town or in the gardens which stretch upstream for nearly half a mile. Behind the market place and parallel to the main street in which stands the Hotel Post runs a narrow street called the König Karl Strasse. A footwalk shaded by young lime trees borders the river, and on the railings along the stream boxes of flowers have been placed overhanging the water of a long pool dammed up by a sluice at its lower end. The water is very clear, and beside the footpath and under the back walls of the houses across the stream trout of all sizes can be seen swimming idly against the current. Some, under the rails on the street side, lie close to the surface, well aware of their immunity and in no way embarrassed by passers-by who lean on the rails to watch them and drop crumbs which they rise to inspect and sometimes condescend to eat. At the upper end of the König Karl Strasse one enters the Town Gardens. Here is white rushing water with deep holes among the rocks, rippling shallows and wide eddying pools. From the paths and bridges you can see trout of all sizes, some very large, swimming in the shallows or in the rocky pools, appearing and disappearing as they move, now in the calm water at the edge, and now in the greater depths of the main stream as it flows, lightly tinged with brown and dappled with the sunlight which falls through the early leaves of overhanging beech and elm.

The sight of all these trout in and immediately above the town disposed at once of all fear that the occupation forces or other hazards had emptied the river of fish and made it seem certain that in the miles of water above the gardens we would find plenty. So to the upper water we now pinned our hopes and turned our thoughts. In the 5 miles of the valley which stretch upstream between Wildbad and the small village of Enzklösterle lie groups of scattered houses, small farms at the edge of the forest and sawmills beside the river. To serve these, a few infrequent buses pass up and down the valley, and though their times of running are calculated to meet the needs of the workers rather than the convenience of the fisherman, they can, with suitable planning, be made to serve the latter. So on the day following our fruitless expedition below the town, we ate an early breakfast of coffee, rolls and honey and took the 8.15 am bus two miles up to the little inn which stands beside the foresters' houses at Christofshof. Heavy dew was on the grass as we walked across the meadow to the river.

The Enz at the point to which we had come is a rapid stream, shallow for the most part, but with deeper runs and a few pools in places where the water has eaten in, under or around the roots of overhanging trees. I find it hard to compare the volume of one river with that of another, but it seemed to us that in size the Enz at this point was not unlike the stretch of the Aberdeenshire Don near the village of Strathdon, a little smaller than the Deveron above Huntly. It was, in any event, a stream which could be easily fished with the light trout rods we had with us. The water was crystal clear and in the shallows trout in reassuring numbers were plainly visible. On the near side, a belt of rich meadow land stretched downstream to a bend of the river, irrigated by little ditches the courses of which were marked by lush grass and water plants. Across the stream the forest came down to the waterside and here at first was our undoing; for as surely as the flow of the water had formed a little pool or a run of some depth, so surely when we tried to fish it, did we find that overhanging branches of fir or beech, alder or willow bending in places almost to the water had formed a trellis in which our most cunning and circumspect attempts to cast ended in frustration or disaster. Signs of the winter's floods were everywhere apparent. Floating twigs and dead grass had caught in the branches of the overhanging trees, while bunches of flotsam and winter's debris trapped in the eddies filled and ruined many a promising spot. A short way downstream we came on a small party of foresters repairing the winter's damage. In the shallow water, stones and large gravel had been placed in long sausage-shaped rolls of heavy netting and these had been laid as a breakwater along the base of the bank. On the face of the bank itself netting had been pinned into the ground and over it was laid a covering of willow shoots, the thicker ends covered with a thin sprinkling of earth and dried peat to help them to root. The work was neatly

and effectively done for the protection of the meadow land, but it had
little value to the fisherman for whom the natural hazards of the
waterside would remain, to be faced as best he could.

At the foot of the meadow the trees on both sides of the valley closed
in on the stream and where it entered the forest we lunched, chastened
and frustrated. Now our troubles were multiplied. Trees in front and
behind and branches overhead defied efforts which grew increasingly
despairing, and as the day wore on a sense of complete inadequacy and
a feeling that Nature and all else was against us grew almost over-
powering. Pools which, in a more rational frame of mind, would have
been approached and attacked with hope and success were abandoned
with hardly a glance, and evening found us in the meadows above the
town ready to give up a seemingly fruitless struggle which had cost us
serious loss in flies, casts and self-esteem and which had, after all our
efforts, resulted in the capture of only three trout little if at all over the
size limit of 10 inches. When later that evening, we reviewed the
situation, we debated cynically whether it was better to be able to cast
freely in water where there were no fish, as on the first day, or not to
be able to cast in water where there were many.

Looking back on it all from a distance of time and in the knowledge
of later success, I feel little doubt that our troubles arose partly from the
fact that we were still far more tired at the start of our holiday than we
realised, that we had come fresh and inexperienced to face conditions
which were undeniably difficult, and partly to the fact that we had been
unlucky in choosing for our first day above the town a part of the river
which even later we found relatively unproductive. All this could be
remedied by time, patience and growing knowledge; and so it proved.

No one could for long remain depressed in those spring days with
trees and flowers, meadows and stream in all the beauty of a German
May, and a new day brought new plans and new hopes. Among the
many boxes of flies and casts which I had brought to Germany was a
small cardboard box containing an assortment of large dry flies. These
had been acquired some years before to float for the benefit and entice-
ment of sea-trout on the broad waters of Loch Maree. In size and
colour they resembled no insect likely to be seen on the River Enz and

for that matter few that one would ever see on Loch Maree; but among them by a happy chance were a very few Greenwell's Glories of a size rather larger than one would normally use for brown trout, but tied with stiff hackles to make them buoyant. Now of all the streams I have ever fished at home or abroad, I can recall few, if any, where the Greenwell's Glory could not be used with profit and success. If I were forced to choose one fly and one fly only with which to fish for brown trout in any water at any part of the season, I should without hesitation choose the masterpiece which Canon Greenwell evolved so many years ago. As I lay in bed that night living over again our hard and ill-rewarded day and seeing again those pools under the trees many of which we had too readily passed by as impossible, the thought grew to conviction that surely it would be possible to find some where with care a single fly could be cast with a short line upstream. I saw in fancy a large hackled Greenwell floating on even the rough water of the Enz and the trout welcoming it as they had on other streams in other lands.

Another warm and cloudless morning saw us hurrying through the town gardens bound for the meadows above and the stretch of the river which had witnessed our final admission of defeat the day before. Today as I write, I fancy I can recall in every detail the pool where the dreams and hopes of the night became realities: a long pool deepening towards the rapid water of the neck, but with a broad shallow at the downstream end. Cherry trees fringed it on the near side and hung far out over the water, while alder and willow grew thick on the far bank; but over part of the pool there was clear space. The shallow water of the tail came perilously near and sometimes over the tops of our short rubber boots, but with care it proved possible to reach a point from which an upstream cast could be made. That pool changed our whole outlook. It was full of trout, and though the last few yards of deep water in the neck proved out of our reach and the overhanging cherries successfully guarded a particularly attractive stretch of deep water under the near bank, we had caught five trout before we left it. It is true that two of them were undersized and had to be returned, and of the other three, only one was much over $\frac{1}{2}$lb; but now we felt that the battle was won and that on other pools in the five miles of water above us we could succeed again.

Through the meadows which lie immediately above Wildbad the course of the River Enz is narrow and rapid. Pools of any size are few, and between them the stream flows at a speed which calls for rapid casting lest the line be swept under the trees and bushes of the waterside. The banks, save in a very few places, are thickly fringed with alder, birch and willow and there are many stretches where one can do nothing but look with longing through the leaves at tempting but unfishable water and hurry on to the next fishable place. In such conditions the progress of our education was somewhat painful and attended by loss of temper and tackle, but as time went on we graduated slowly from the status of complete novices, through steady apprenticeship, and if we never quite attained the stature of craftsmen we came, I think, at least within reasonable distance of it. Perhaps the best measure of our progress lies in the fact that while our first two days on the upper river cost us three casts and many flies, the losses from then on were almost negligible and of the five precious Greenwells with which we started, two came back with us from Germany to float on other waters.

With growing knowledge of the stream we learned to recognise those spots where it was possible to guide our rods through the bushes on the bank and, standing precariously on stones at the edge or in the fast stream, to cast with short lines either downstream with wet fly or upstream with dry. For as time went on we found that both methods were effective, though here as elsewhere it seemed that the better trout came to the floating fly. We learned to cast with our thoughts if not our eyes on the trees behind and on either side, and in places where normal casting was impossible, to use a switch cast; but we never mastered the art of striking sideways. This caused us much tribulation, and time and again a sudden unsuccessful strike at a rising trout was followed by ten minutes of exasperation as we struggled to disentangle line, cast and flies from branches overhead, often too high and too distant to be reached. Towards evening on that hard but instructive day, we suffered what at the time we felt to be a major disaster. We had come on a long pool deepening slowly towards its head, full of trout, some of which were rising to natural flies. Someone with an eye to the picturesque had cut the alders on the near bank leaving only a few tall ones nicely spaced along the side. The water was too deep to wade and we had no choice but to cast as best we could from the spaces of open bank between the trees. After a short trial we were tempted to the conclusion that the tree-cutting had been done by a local tackle maker with an eye to business; but by now we had learned circumspection, and even here our efforts were not unrewarded and attended by no loss of flies till growing over-confident I was tempted to hazard one of our few remaining Greenwells on a long cast up into the rapid water. A trout rose. I struck unsuccessfully and then turned to see my precious fly firmly tied round an alder branch high up and overhanging the river. In trying to free it the cast broke. The tree proved unclimbable and in a final effort to retrieve the dangling cast with a rod top, we succeeded in freeing it from the branch only to see it fall far out into the stream and disappear on the fast current.

Up till now our fishing above the town had been confined to the 2 miles between Wildbad and Christofshof; but now we went farther afield and a few days later the early morning bus set us down at a sawmill 5 miles upstream. The warmth of the past few days had brought a rapid change to the valley and in these high meadows 1,500 feet above the sea the flowers of early summer were beginning to appear while those of spring were not yet past. Along the river bank and among the boulders the kingcups still flowered in golden masses such as I have seldom seen. Tall blue forget-me-nots overhung the edge of every ditch, while under the willows and alders at the river's edge and in the damp and shady spots grew thick beds of a dark green water plant. Its foliage resembled that of some tall geranium; the flower was not unlike a small white anemone. It was then unfamiliar to us, but later we were able to identify it as white cinquefoil, a water-loving plant, rare in the British Isles, occasionally found in upland meadows of limestone country. We found it in quantities, and the white flowers against the dark green of the leaves in the shady places where it grew were striking, and very lovely. There was campion too and valerian. In the drier places were spikes of bugloss and blue patches of speedwell, and each day we came on more and more of the early orchis. These meadows of the upper Enz are very narrow and in places the forest comes down close to the stream. Under the straight stems stretching up with hardly a branch for 50, 60 and even 70 feet grew feathery moss sprinkled with wood sorrel and many patches of wood anemones, some pure white and some touched with purple. On the more distant wooded slopes the green of pine and fir was broken here and there by the pale green of beech and elm on which the young leaf was fast appearing. On the river banks and beside the tributary streams was the white of wild cherry and all along the valley were clumps and little thickets of what we know as bird cherry hanging with sprays of cream white blossom, smelling of summer,

Here, near the upper limit of the Wildbad water, the stream was smaller and in places more rocky. We came to a sawmill where men were at work guiding long peeled logs down a deep inlet fed from the river. Where the water from the mill fell again into the main stream we hooked a good trout the playing and landing of which caused a welcome diversion for the men working at the mill. Below the mill the ground fell steeply. The stream tumbled among large boulders overhung with trees; and here we lunched. When we started again I discovered that the check on my reel had gone and on unscrewing the side of the reel I found that the metal ratchet had snapped across. My spare reels were 5 miles off at Wildbad, so there was nothing for it but to fish out the rest of the day as best I could, checking and recovering the line by hand. It was singularly inopportune that the next trout, one of our best, was foul-hooked in a tiny pool behind a boulder at the head of a long series of rapids. It exploited to the utmost a situation full of possibilities, and after a hazardous scramble along the rocky bank with the trout far downstream, I counted myself lucky to be able to guide it at last into quiet water and the net; but from the broken reel came in the end advantage. On my return to Scotland I took the reel to be mended. I then learned for the first time in nearly fifty years of fishing that very many of Messrs Hardy's reels including that which I had been using are provided with a spare spring and ratchet placed alongside that in normal use—an elementary piece of knowledge, the earlier possession of which would have saved me a harassing afternoon on the upper Enz.

Throughout the rest of the day we fished our way slowly down the valley, crossing and recrossing the river on the rough wooden bridges made by the foresters, tempting Providence beside many a rocky and overgrown pool, sometimes, but not always, with impunity. For with growing practice the odds against us tended to shorten and our baskets to fill. Late in the day we came to a rough seat in a meadow at the edge of the forest and here we sat to rest and count our twenty trout before leaving the river. None of the trout were over ¾lb and the average was only about ½lb but they were lovely fish, thickly spotted, the red spots rather more numerous and prominent than on those of Scottish streams. In this second week of May they had not yet come to the finest condition which another few weeks of summer feeding would give them, but for strength and vigour we could hardly have asked for better. The coffee of the Waldluft Gasthaus was excellent and as we drank it, waiting for the bus and sharing the last remnants of our lunch with the proprietor's friendly labrador, we looked back on a happy day.

The mystery of the silent pools below Wildbad still remained unsolved, but the striking contrast between the stretch above the town and that below and the fact that the Little Enz which flows in at Calmbach was full of trout narrowed the field for speculation and led us in the end to what seemed the inescapable conclusion. None the less, the recollection of the lower river as it had been before the war still haunted me, and on a warm sunny day soon after our success far up the valley, I took the train to Calmbach. The apple trees beside the station were now in full blossom and the brown roofs of the village showed through a bank of white and pink and red as I made for the lower meadows. At the foot of a steep beech wood is a lovely deep pool, its upper half overhung on the far side by a tall fir. It seemed the very place for a big trout and indeed on my pre-war visits to Wildbad it had been very productive; but though I watched for long beside it, and then floated a fly at random again and again, there was no sign of life. Moving upstream I came to the tail of a long smooth run. The water flowed deep but with a good flow under the grass and willows of the banks;

and here I lit a pipe and waited. Presently there came that sound, as of the bursting of a bubble, familiar to all dry fly fisherman. It came again and now I could see a trout feeding steadily close under the far bank. It seemed large, and though far across the stream appeared to present no insuperable problem. After a few preliminary casts my fly fell right and though it dragged slightly, the trout rose but did not take hold. This made no difference to the steady feeding of the trout which seemed to be taking all that passed over him. During the next hour I tried him at intervals, changing the fly again and again with fingers which shook with excitement and impatience as he fed steadily on; but he would have none of it, and though I changed position I could not avoid the drag caused by the long line crossing the intervening current. At length I decided to give him up, but he rose again very slightly lower, and casting again I hooked him. He felt heavy and sluggish and had I not seen him, I would have thought him to be a chub; but he was a trout and a good one. He got far below me and when he turned sideways to the current as I held him I saw that he was foul-hooked somewhere in the gill cover. Despite this, he had little enterprise and allowed himself to be slowly pulled upstream. He was near the net when the hold gave, but not before I had seen that he was badly diseased in the head and also it seemed near the tail. This had not affected his appetite, but it is sometimes so with sick or injured trout. I did not regret his escape after a moral defeat, but as I walked home to Wildbad, having seen nothing more, I felt growing concern for the future of the lower river, and looked with no friendly thoughts at the paper factory below the town which at times discharges its waste into the river. The factory had been at work when I fished there long before the war and the trout then seemed none the worse; but twenty years of continuous, if spasmodic pollution, had taken place since then. Was my trout a last survivor fighting a gallant but losing battle for existence? I greatly feared so.

The plan of the river printed on the back of our permits showed that the part of the stream through the town where fishing was not allowed ended at certain sluice gates where the main stream could be diverted for the use of the paper factory. The bed of the stream between these gates and the discharge from the factory several hundred yards below was usually almost dry except for a few still deep pools, which in that state were quite unfishable; but when the gates were open the whole stream came through and at one point there was a deep run close under the steep wall of the neighbouring roadway. Here, occasionally, we saw big trout rising, but the pool was not fishable from the roadside wall which fell sheer to the water, and the opposite bank could not be reached; but one evening returning from a fruitless expedition downstream I found that though work at the factory had ended, the sluice gates had, by some chance, been left only partially open so that a portion only of the stream passed down the main channel. This made it possible even with short rubber boots to wade across and fish the roadside pool from the far bank. The tail and centre of the pool were very still, but in the neck there was a short stretch of rough water and into this, as I waded up, the trout gradually retired. Perhaps they felt safe to continue feeding there and almost certainly they had seldom been fished for. A small crowd quickly collected on the edge of the road above, and leaning over the roadside railings they must have had an interesting view of my fly floating over the trout almost directly below them. Two trout were quickly caught and great enthusiasm greeted the hooking of a much larger third one. It played strongly far up in the rough water and was finally and precariously landed with the inexpert assistance of one of the audience who waded across to help and who was only with difficulty restrained from trying to pull it ashore by means of the cast. It weighed 1½lb and was the largest trout we caught during our time at Wildbad in 1956.

When the roadside pool was exhausted, my enthusiastic friend led me by a devious and difficult route up the bed of the river to a point directly below the sluice gates. Here were two deep pools full of trout of all sizes. One of about 1lb I caught on a floating fly, but though my German friend urged me to continue and even found some worms, which I have no doubt would have proved deadly, I felt little interest in fishing in what was little more than an aquarium. I had, too, an uneasy feeling that if someone had discovered that the sluice gates had not been properly opened and had come to remedy this omission, our

position immediately below them and enclosed on either side by
unclimbable walls would have been at least awkward.

Considering what store the Germans set by trout, it seems surprising
that the art of fishing for them is apparently so little practised. Every
hotel has its tank where you can choose your trout for dinner, and all
up and down the valleys are hatcheries and fish ponds. In the valley of
the Enz, at some points within a few hundred yards of where we were
fishing, was the great highroad from Stuttgart to Freudenstadt. The
sound of traffic rarely ceased; but beside the river so close at hand we
might have been in a different world in company only with the stream,
the trees and flowers, the water ouzels and the wagtails. It is true that
very occasionally, we saw in the distance Germans on the river using
long rods and what were palpably baits of various sorts despite the
peremptory rules to the contrary; but only once did we meet serious
fishermen. It was in a meadow a short way above the town that we
came on them; two men wearing long lacing boots, checked shirts and
long-peaked caps. They seemed embarrassed when they saw us coming
in the distance and made some hurried adjustments to their lines. We
exchanged some remarks—in halting German on our part, and in
something quite unintelligible on theirs—but this led to no useful result
and further progress seemed unlikely till some familiar intonation in
their speech gave us a clue and led to the discovery that our friends were
American airmen stationed near Stuttgart. Their tiny rods were little
more than tokens, but equipped with complex and costly reels. At the
end of their lines were short lengths of thick gut. Attached to these,
one was using what looked like a miniature beetle of sinister appearance taken from a large assortment of insects and minnows which he
carried in a metal box, each more lifelike than the last. The other had
a large red fly, kept afloat, he explained, by a small celluloid ball on the
gut cast. This he told us could be filled with water as required to reg-
ulate the depth of the fly in the water. They had also, as they later
confessed, a tin of worms for use should the products of modern science
fail them. They had caught little, and shortly after we parted, their
large car passed down the road giving us a farewell hoot and leaving

us to the peace of the river and our out-moded but not unsuccessful methods.

The possibilities of the upper river seemed almost endless and, as our knowledge grew, we found more and still more places where, with reasonable care and some luck, we could cast a fly; but there were long stretches of stream between the bushes, and many tree-fringed pools which we could never fish; and all were full of trout. In water so strong and rapid the rise of a trout was almost invariably sudden and impetuous, and time and again it found us unprepared. This was as true of the floating fly as of the sunk. It was seldom possible to float a dry fly over a particular trout as on a chalk stream or on a smoother flowing river. The fly had to be floated over every likely spot and especially where overhanging branches shaded the deeper parts of the stream. Often we would lose sight of the small fly in the rapid water; but if the sunlight fell on the water and the light was good, the fly could be plainly seen and I know few things more fascinating than watching that tiny speck of brown come sailing down, bobbing and pitching on the little waves, its life in its hands, chancing its luck.

As the days passed, the gold of the kingcups faded. The cherry blossom too was past the peak of its glory and from the riverside trees white petals fell and drifted on the stream below; but in the meadows new buds and new flowers appeared each day among the grass, and all up and down the valley, spring and summer were meeting. Our time at Wildbad was fast running out. Each morning we would start off for the meadows above the gardens or in the early bus to the upper valley, returning after long days tired but contented. To the well-dressed Germans taking their evening walk through the gardens, we must have been a constant source of wonder as we made our way homeward bearing all the marks of a hard day by the river; but our rods acted to some degree as passports, and though I think we remained to the last something of an enigma, cold stares of disapproval would change to smiles of somewhat puzzled tolerance, if not of complete understanding. On these late spring evenings the square in front of the hotel was quiet when we returned, save for the swifts which wheeled and screamed round the tower of the old church where the golden hands told on the blue face of the clock the passing hours. As we turned in to the Hotel Post, Adolf would greet us with a smile of anticipation and would hurry off to the kitchen to count and weigh the catch, the greater part of which was, to their continuing astonishment, later shared between himself and our other friend, the head waiter.

The last fishing day came. All through a grey and sunless morning, we fished the lower meadows with small success. Towards midday, we made once more for the upper meadows walking up as far as the foresters' houses at Christofshof. Here the Enz is joined on its right bank by a small stream which runs through the narrow meadows of a little glen from which the forest rises steeply on either side. A woodmen's road crosses the main river and passing under sycamore trees leads into the glen. On a sheltered bank beside the bridge we sat to eat our lunch. The sun was breaking through the clouds; peacock butterflies were appearing and flies started to hatch. All through the growing warmth of the afternoon we fished our way up the valley finding good trout rising in nearly every pool. When late in the day in a little meadow below a sawmill we sat to count our seventeen trout, we felt that this, our last day, had been perhaps our best.

Back at the Waldluft Gasthaus we looked for the last time across the meadows to the river. Below us cows, loosed from the evening milking, grazed among the apple trees of a farm orchard. A string of white geese came up the meadow from the waterside, and across the gleaming river the tall firs on the west-facing slopes of the forest threw lengthening shadows on green moss and blaeberry. As we waited for the distant post-horn of the approaching bus, I looked back on more than twenty years. The shadow over the land had passed. The quietness of the valley and the happiness of the fisherman had come again.

CHAPTER 7

On a Welsh trout stream

During the winter of 1956, my wife and I learned that a business engagement was likely to take us to St Helier in Jersey during the last days of May in the coming year. The Channel Islands do not number among their charms any facilities for the trout fisher, and the impending engagement did not initially turn our minds to fishing; but as the winter passed and the first stirrings of an early spring came to Scotland our thoughts began to stray down fascinating if disturbing paths. In Jersey we would be almost a stone's throw from the Continent, and soon we were toying with thoughts of the streams of South Germany, Austria and the Pyrenees. The more ambitious plans were soon discarded on grounds of time, distance and cost, but for several weeks we considered more seriously the idea of visiting that part of Belgium which borders on the German frontier. Here in the wooded limestone hills of the Belgian Ardennes was surely a promising field for exploration with a trout rod. A detailed map of the Ardennes showed a multitude of small streams forming the headwaters of the rivers Semois and Lesse which run to the Meuse, and when we found that nearly all the hotels in the small towns and villages of that district

F

advertised fishing prominently among their attractions it seemed that there indeed was a paradise waiting for us.

During the next few weeks we corresponded with a number of hotels and local travel agencies with results which were almost entirely negative. The replies we received to our letters made it abundantly clear that Belgian hotel-keepers and Belgian travel agencies know little of trout fishing as we understand it, and that if we went to the Ardennes our journey must be directed by faith and hope rather than by any reliable information. With ample time and a car at one's disposal such a trip would have been interesting and very possibly fruitful; but with only a bare fortnight to spare, and with the idea of taking our car with us ruled out by the Jersey visit, the uncertainties were too great, and with some regret we turned our thoughts elsewhere.

Those who used to read the *Fishing Gazette* will recall that in it appeared in the spring months of each year many advertisements of hotels with fishing rights in the south-western counties of England and in Wales. Among those which appeared in the spring of 1957 was an advertisement of the Talbot Inn at Tregaron in Cardiganshire. Fishing in many miles of Association Water in the River Teifi was said to be available, and after a study of the map and some preliminary enquiries we decided to explore what for us was an unknown district and arranged to go to Tregaron after our visit to the Channel Islands.

It almost seemed that our ignorance of Tregaron was shared by British Railways, for when at Paddington some weeks later we asked that our luggage be labelled for that place, it was only after some research that the necessary labels could be produced, while our impression that Tregaron was not a common place of resort was strengthened by the fact that, when at last found, the labels bore a spelling different from that on the maps of today. The old Great Western Railway out of Paddington is surely one of the most pleasant routes out of London. My journeys by it usually take me by Reading and Newbury and up the Kennet Valley, giving thrilling glimpses of the Kennet now on one side and now on the other with sometimes the sight of a rising trout, and so, by the side of the old canal, over the watershed to the dairy farms and the thatched cottages of Somerset. But today we branched off at Reading into the green rolling country of Wiltshire and Gloucestershire, and beyond the Severn the crowds and bustle of Newport, Swansea and Cardiff alternated and contrasted with lovely views of the Welsh coast line and the silver expanse of Carmarthen Bay.

To reach Tregaron from the south, we had to change at Carmarthen on to the branch line which climbs steeply from the coast. All around was the fresh green and the flowers of early summer. On the steep sides of the wooded glen above the estuary of the Towy the oaks were already almost in full leaf, and in the deep cuttings ferns, herb robert and wild strawberries hanging from the rock face seemed almost to brush the windows of our train as we passed, with campion and cranesbill on the fringes of the woods. Beyond the watershed we came into a wide valley and looked down on the bends of the river, the upper reaches of which we had come to fish.

The little market town of Tregaron lies at the foot of a small valley through which a mountain stream, the Berlyn, flows to join the River Teifi. It is a green valley, for this is mainly dairy country, and beside the stream on either side is a network of small pasture fields enclosed by high hedges of hawthorn and hazel, blackthorn and wild rose. On the higher ground and far up towards the head of the valley nestle little remote white farms, their only access narrow lanes deep sunk and wandering between steep banks of ferns and wild flowers. At the head of the valley of the Berlyn the hills rise green to the sky-line, and beyond is high trackless country rising to 2,000 feet and more and stretching with hardly a break to the valley of the upper Wye, 30 miles to the east.

The Talbot Inn at Tregaron is a low cream-washed building of great age. The local people put the date of part of the building as early as 1100, and certainly the deeply worn slate slabs which pave the ground floor passages tell of the traffic of very many generations. In the low ceiling of the dining-room which, when we were there, showed traces of more ancient use as a kitchen, massive oak beams black with age projected from cream coloured plaster. If the reported date of the building was at all accurate—and certainly on every side were signs of great antiquity—it seemed not impossible that these great beams had been cut from oak trees which were seedlings when Alfred ruled in Wessex. The low square windows of the inn look out through 4-foot thick walls to the square of the little town where for most of the week there is little traffic to disturb the old men who smoke and take their ease on the wooden benches which surround the central statue of some local celebrity. Only on Saturdays and on market days is the square busy, when farmers from the hills come down to sell their beasts or to do their frugal shopping, the younger men on tractors, the older on shaggy ponies.

The Teifi rises in the hills some eight miles to the north of Tregaron. After leaving the high ground the stream enters a great expanse of flat boggy ground which stretches downstream almost to Tregaron. The upper part of this boggy ground is a Nature Reserve. It has been well chosen. Here are more than three square miles of peat in one of Britain's best developed raised bogs, the breeding place of over seventy species of birds and the only regular wintering ground in southern Britain for the Greenland white-fronted goose. From the stone bridge on the road to Aberystwyth which crosses the bog near its lower end, one looks north over five miles of reeds and rushes and bog grass where the winding river has cut its way through the peat, giving here and there glimpses of open water where the sunlight is reflected from deep pools. Beyond the bog are low wooded hills where in 1164 the Cistercian monks built their monastery; but in the foreground nothing breaks the great expanse where in spring and summer curlew wheel and call continuously, while buzzards from the hills, soaring overhead, look down on the windings of the stream where the wild things of the bog-lands live their lives undisturbed and almost inaccessible. Not even the cattle which graze with impunity in the marshy ground farther downstream and know well the crossings of the river venture on to the treacherous ground of the upper bog.

On the morning following our arrival at Tregaron the local banker, with a readiness which suggested that business in that line had not been brisk, supplied us with weekly fishing tickets, to be renewed at the start of our second week. These entitled us to fish on no less than 12 miles of water controlled by the local fishing association; so it was clear that failure to catch fish would, at least, not be due to lack of scope for the practice of our art. But even as we bought our tickets we had to own to a growing fear that success might not be lightly achieved. Before coming to Tregaron we had made what enquiry we could about the river and had learned that in these upper reaches it was mainly a trout stream, but with some salmon and sea-trout in the late summer and autumn. So we had brought several trout rods and one sea-trout rod, though in the event the latter never left its case. For Wales was suffering from one of the exceptional droughts which seem so often to coincide with our fishing holidays, and no rain had fallen for several weeks. Below the bog where the river flowed briskly the streams were pathetically thin, while on the slower stretches and in the bog itself only the slight movement of underwater weeds showed that a current was moving.

Then began a succession of days of frustration and some disappointment. There was no lack of trout, for we could see them in the pools and shallows, while in some of the deeper pools below Tregaron there were even a very few salmon, suffering no doubt the same feelings of frustration as we ourselves. But to get trout to come to a fly seemed almost hopeless. In the streams, such trout as were feeding lay in only a few inches of the clearest water, where even the finest nylon must, to judge from their reactions, have seemed to them like cable. In the deeper pools where the water seemed less clear the fly moved so slowly that any trout at all interested had ample time to make the most minute inspection and reach the right conclusion.

A local bus maintains a service on the side road which follows the east bank of the Teifi and leads from Tregaron to the larger town of Lampeter 10 miles downstream. Its hours of departure have been fixed without due regard to the needs of the fisherman. But for all that, it came to serve our purpose reasonably well, and after a hard apprenticeship we learned to pronounce, sufficiently well to be intelligible to the driver, the names of local places and particularly that of the tiny hamlet of Lanndewi Brefi to which we often went. Here a narrow side road leads down to the river which it crosses at the stone bridge of Gogoyan. Below the bridge the Teifi runs for a short way among willow bushes, the bends of the stream forming deep pools of some apparent promise. These culminate in a long pool where the water is partially dammed back by the remains of a broken weir once used to divert water to a nearby mill; and here, abandoning the upper streams as hopeless in the prevailing conditions, we often came. The early bus by which we sometimes travelled, would drop us at the road end long before the heat of the day had brought the hope of hatching flies and rising trout, and with ample time on our hands we would not hurry over our short walk to the river. It was a pleasant prelude to the day. On either side of the sunken lane the steep banks, topped by hedges of stunted oak and hazel or dwarf walls of stone and slate were bright with the flowers and foliage of late spring and early summer. There was campion and foxglove, speedwell, violet and anemone, with spleenwort and hart's tongue ferns in the shady places and valerian growing in the walls, and in the hedges above were tangles of honeysuckle, bramble and wild rose. If the brilliant weather was cheating us of the full water which we needed so much, at least it was offering us compensation on every side. Beside the river, too, we seemed to be fishing almost in a flower garden. The kingcups, though past their best, were still in flower, with clumps of mimulus among the stones. In the river itself, except in the few deep wide pools, the channels of open water, already shrunk by the drought, had been still further narrowed by spreading beds of water buttercup. I recall in particular one wide and shallower stretch where the beds on either side had met. Looking from below one saw far upstream the sparkle of light on a few yards of running water before it was lost to view beneath an unbroken sheet of the white and gold blossoms of the covering weed.

These were some of the compensations for the defeated fisherman; and the birds too played their full part. Now, with the growing foliage of early summer thickening on every tree and bush, it was becoming each day more difficult to distinguish the small birds whose song and movement was always around us as we fished. One family of wrens I recall of which we had a close and almost domestic view. The whole family, four young birds and their parents had been unwittingly but most rudely disturbed by us in a hawthorn bush and were determined to let us know what they thought of our intrusion. The parents scolded as only wrens can, while the young birds, each about the size of a walnut and hardly yet able to fly, hopped from twig to twig letting us see and hear that, if their education in flying was yet incomplete, their schooling in the use of invective had already reached an advanced stage. Over the river the sand-pipers and water ouzels were, as always, our constant fishing companions; herons when disturbed flapped slowly from one fishing ground to the next, and when we sat to rest or eat our lunch there were few moments when the sky did not hold plover and curlew or, far up, buzzards from the surrounding hills.

The day we saw the wrens I had one piece of bad luck, followed later by good luck, the recollection of which still gives me some pleasure. We had gone far downstream to a part of the river which, till then, we had seldom visited. Here in a long wide pool I found what seemed a good trout rising in fairly rapid water under the far bank. Unluckily, hawthorn bushes overhung the water at this point and there was only one angle from which the fish could be reached, and that only with a long cast. The local farmers, in their efforts to keep their cattle from the stream shared with the bus owners a regrettable disregard for the interests of the fisherman. The pool in question was a case in point, for at the precise spot and distance which the back cast of one fishing a dry fly up into the stream would reach, two strands of barbed wire had been stretched. I noted the barbed wire and determined to avoid it; but the sight of a good trout rising is apt to be destructive of good resolutions, and as I made my final cast I felt the slight check and snap so familiar to us all, and my line came forward without the fly. Reeling in with some justified annoyance I went back to the offending fence to search, regretting that my fly book contained only scissors and not wire-cutters. I searched thoroughly but vainly, and concluding at last that the spring of the nylon on the wire had jerked the fly to a distance I gave it up and wrote that trout off as unassailable, since I had no wish to risk a repetition. Two days later we again passed the pool and again

a good trout was rising in the very same place. By now the bitterness
of my previous experience had been somewhat allayed, and determined
that I would not again fall a victim to past indiscretion I resolved to
try again from the same spot; and indeed no other was possible.
With the position of the barbed wire clear in my mind's eye I slowly
and carefully made my preliminary casts. As I did so the trout rose again,
slightly farther off than I had expected, and all caution deserted me.
I made the final long cast. Again I felt the tension and heard the snap
behind me, and my cast came forward without the fly. Readers of
these pages may have noted that the Greenwell's Glory is of all dry
flies my favourite. I never seem to have enough of them, and this
further disaster threatened to rob me of yet another of a dwindling
stock of a fly to which I was—or should I in the circumstances say,
had been?—closely attached. This time I was determined to recover
it, so without reeling in I repeated the cast several times without the
fly with the object of noting exactly where the back cast would reach
the fence. Having noted this as closely as possible I walked back to the
fence. There, precisely where I had expected it was my Greenwell's
Glory caught in the wire, and four inches from it was the fly lost two
days before.

   Hitherto, we had fished the river only by day, but as our time at
Tregaron was drawing to an end with no sign of rain we decided,
rather in desperation than in real hope, to fish late at night. Only one
pool seemed suitable for this—the pool above the weir near the bridge
at Gogoyan, wide and deep and free of trees; and here one evening we
came just before the light began to fail. A few small trout were rising,
but we sat waiting in the hope that a real rise would start. A few flies
were on the water, but nothing approaching a real hatch. Quite suddenly the air was full of small white midges, covering the banks and
the pool almost like a mist. The trout seemed to go mad, and from
comparative calm the surface of the pool in a moment became covered
with the splash and ripple of rising fish. We tried everything we could
think of, dry fly and wet, but all to no purpose. We got, it is true,
one or two very small trout; but nothing of any size showed any
interest in us, though some of those which were feeding so greedily

seemed really large. Our only consolation was that the midges did not bite us; but then neither did the trout, and we felt we would have gladly suffered the tortures of the Skye midge at its worst in return for some real interest on the part of the trout. The hatch, as so often happens, disappeared as suddenly as it had come, and soon we were making our way up the lane to the waiting car, taking what consolation we could—and indeed it was more than a little—from the smell of honeysuckle in the wayside hedges, a full moon over the hills and the soft air of a perfect June night.

The last days of our stay at Tregaron followed the pattern so sadly familiar to us from fishing expeditions on the West Coast of Scotland. Two days before we were due to leave torrential rain fell. All through that night it rained hard, and next day the river was in huge and muddy flood. Gone were the white and gold beds of weed, the kingcups and the mimulus, taking with them much of the character and loveliness of the river. The rain passed as suddenly as it had come and on our last day the level of the stream was falling fast; but the mud and debris washed down after weeks of drought had probably sickened the trout, and even large wet flies met with no response.

The day of our departure was warm and sunny, and as our train ran down the valley to Carmarthen and the coast we could see that the river had fallen to a perfect fishing level, and here and there we could even see trout starting to rise. It seemed hard to be leaving it all when success seemed at last so near; but as he grows older, though the pleasure in catching trout or the sense of regret and disappointment at failure may be little less keen, the fisherman comes to place a higher value on his surroundings as he fishes, the trees and flowers and birds, the light on moving water and all the countless things which go to make up the enduring pleasure of fishing. So it was with us as we left Tregaron. As the train took us from the white sands and wide estuaries of the Welsh coast, beyond the Severn to the pastures and hay fields below the Downs, and at last to London, we thought less of the trout we had not caught but increasingly of the green flowery lanes winding to the river, the water buttercups all in blossom, and the green folds of the hills looking down on that quiet valley.

CHAPTER 8

Dry fly in the hills

It was the third week of May. Far up on the north side of the Ochils where my home lies we had wakened to thick mist blowing in from the Tay estuary and the North Sea. Throughout most of the morning the mist persisted, but towards midday the sun began to struggle through, promising a warm afternoon. During the last few days a moderate amount of rain had fallen and the hill streams, of which the Ochils have so many, were full though not in spate. The early spring months had been cold, uninviting and unpromising for the trout fisherman; but now, as late spring merged into summer, thoughts of trout, natural flies and waterside flowers had come flooding back, and with them the urge to be again beside the burns. More than this, the northeast wind which had blown the mist in from the coast would, I knew, be blowing up the glen I meant to visit, favouring the technique I had in mind. So, putting a 9½ foot dry fly rod with casts and dry flies and a pair of thigh waders into the back of the car, I took the road which leads back into the hills.

A group of ancient ash trees marking, with scattered stones, the site of some old farm buildings stands between the road and the stream, and here I left the car. At this point some two miles from the top of the glen the burn has reached a sufficient size to make fly fishing just possible, though it is, as yet, only a small stream. Half a mile farther down, however, it is joined by another stream of about equal size, and from this point onwards, at least when the stream is full, it is of fair size though still nothing more than a large hill burn.

This is a burn which I have fished repeatedly as a boy, as a young man and now (1957) after more than fifty years of fishing, as one not so young. During most of these years it has been my habit to fish it with small wet flies and generally down the stream. But that day conditions were favourable for the different method which I mean to try.

As I came through the clump of old ash trees a cuckoo was saying clearly and monotonously to all around that it was May and that he had come to stay. Black-faced ewes and their lambs were busy grazing on the lush spring grass beside the trees—the lambs already learning to nibble like their parents, but when disturbed forgetting their dignity and rushing for the comfort of mother and the dairy. Along the hillside a little way up from the burn runs a clearly marked path, once the route of the postman on his rounds, but now used only by sheep and an occasional shepherd; and this I followed. Below me the burn ran, as I had hoped and expected, full and with the least touch of brown. I passed the junction of the two burns, looking down on the ruins of the cottages which stood there in days long past when men and women worked—with what infinite labour—the small fields, the outlines of which are still to be seen far up the hillsides. Beside the path pansies and wild violets were showing among the grass which would soon be sprinkled with the gold of tormentil and the white of woodruff. Across the glen on the steep slopes of the opposite hillside the whin was a golden mass. Below me the hazels and rowans beside the burn were already green, but on the ash trees (late that year) the black buds showed hardly a sign of life.

It was tempting to follow on down the path with so much to see and enjoy on every side, while far downstream the view opened to

Strathearn and the Grampians beyond. But there was only a short afternoon before me and so leaving the path I came down to the burn side and set up my rod. A mile of fishing water lay upstream between me and the car. The wind still blew lightly but steadily upstream. The burn ran full and hope ran high. In place of the usual cast with two small wet flies I took from my cast-case a light tapered nylon cast and on it knotted my old favourite, a small Greenwell's Glory tied with stiff hackles to make it float. It seemed, indeed, a strange place in which to fish with a dry fly, and those dry fly fishermen accustomed only to the broader streams of Scotland or the chalk streams of the south might well have smiled. The stream was in few places more than four yards across, running in a bed filled with stones and small boulders, some moss-covered and others already fringed with the young leaf of the mimulus which would soon be in flower. Among these stones and boulders the stream flowed in swift and shallow runs, deep only here and there under the overhanging banks, or in deep potholes into which the water tumbled in tiny falls through the stones above. Here and there are small pools of some length, but these are exceptional. For the most part the homes of the trout are under the banks at the edge of the shallow streams or in the swirling potholes.

In such a stream the obvious difficulty for the dry fly fisherman is to defeat the drag on the fly after it has landed on the water. All too often the slack of the greased line falls on rapid water and the fly is whisked away almost as soon as it touches the surface. The trout in these hill burns are perhaps not so discriminating as those which live in chalk streams or more placid waters, and will occasionally snap at a fly which is beginning to drag; but even they have their wits about them and a rapidly dragging fly is ignored. Sometimes, as when casting into a pothole beneath a small fall, the drag can be partially avoided by casting the line over a conveniently placed boulder. This keeps much of the casting line out of the water and allows the gut and fly to rest for a few seconds undisturbed. These trout are very quick and if the fly will float for even these few seconds it is enough. Often, however, when casting up a rapid stream, there is no convenient boulder. Here I have found that the most effective plan is to check the cast sharply while the fly is still a foot or more above the water. This causes the fly to rise a little in the air and to fall softly and perpendicularly on the water at the end of a slightly loose line. The loose line and rapid recovery of the slack by hand as the current floats it downstream will often allow the fly to float free and unhurried for the few seconds needed. Each little stream or tiny pool has its problems, some soluble others not; but all are full of interest and, for me, fascination and endless pleasure, and it must be admitted that there is considerable satisfaction in inducing a trout to rise in circumstances in which some degree of skill is needed.

The first few pools which I fished on that May afternoon, though apparently promising and relatively easy, produced nothing and I began to wonder whether something was wrong with the conditions or whether the season was still too early for dry fly fishing on these high hill burns. More likely in my keenness I was fishing hurriedly and carelessly; but after that the luck changed and soon I was catching fish. In such a small stream no large trout are to be looked for even in the few deep pools. A trout of $\frac{1}{2}$lb is a good one and anything much over this rather exceptional; but even a trout of $\frac{1}{4}$lb on a tiny fly and fine cast and a light rod in such rapid water is exciting if one's expectations are geared to the possibilities, and while many of the trout I caught could be and were pulled in with little ceremony not a few were treated with great respect. The first few trout I caught were all under $\frac{1}{4}$lb and were all returned. After that I caught several rather larger ones; but having returned the early ones I decided to keep my standard high, and in the end I returned all I caught, though many were $\frac{1}{4}$lb and a few slightly more.

There will be some who will say that it is a shame to cause needless alarm and perhaps injury to small trout in streams where one knows that few large ones live. To this I can only answer that the alternatives are to content oneself with killing baskets of very small trout, to do as I did, or to give up fishing these hill burns. I would be sorry indeed to abandon what gives so much pleasure, and so for the years during which I can still walk the hills and fish the streams I propose to continue the policy of returning all but the very best of my trout.

As I reflected on the pleasure which these small trout in the hill streams were giving to me, I recalled that within two weeks' time I hoped to be fishing the River Test. How different the conditions would be! The trout would be at least four times the size and almost all clearly visible in deep, clear and mainly placid water. There, as here, the drag on the fly would be my great enemy, and an even more bitter one, for no chalk-stream trout will look twice at a fly which does not float entirely naturally and freely. But the most essential difference, perhaps, would be in the speed of striking. In these hill burns in Scotland one must strike like lightning as soon as any suspicion of a rise is seen. In Hampshire this is fatal. Particularly, where, as so often, the trout is seen coming to the fly, one must wait. On the Test they advocate the counting of three—and not too quickly at that. In the previous year on the Test I had risen many fish but caught few. The methods learned and practised on so many Scottish burns and rivers are not easily modified, and again and again a rising trout would be missed or at best lightly hooked. I was determined that this year on the Test I would profit by the lesson learned on previous visits.

But thoughts of the great trout of the Test did not detract from the pleasure of this spring day among the small trout of the Ochils. Soon I came to a bend in the stream and saw some thirty yards ahead a slow, deep run under a rock face where I remembered having risen an unusually good trout the previous summer. Now I felt hopeful that I would have him; but it was not to be. As I hurried towards the tail of the pool a mallard splashed out from under the bank followed by six ducklings. The Mother set off up the stream trailing both wings to draw me off while the ducklings scattered and disappeared no doubt according to orders. The duck's diversionary manoeuvres took her right through the middle of the deep stream on which I had set my heart and in which she left a wake like a small motor-launch. Though I waited a few minutes and tried the pool when peace again reigned, it was with faint hope and no success.

So I fished slowly and happily up that quiet glen. The trout continued to rise steadily and freely to my floating fly wherever I could contrive to make it float undisturbed for even a few seconds, and had I been killing the trout caught, my basket would by now have been of appreciable weight. The Greenwell with which I had started the afternoon had long since become too tattered for further use. The few natural flies which were hatching in sheltered corners seemed to be of the pale olive type, but I had replaced the Greenwell with a March Brown picked almost at random from my fly box, and the trout seemed to rise equally well to it. Towards evening I came to the junction pool of the two burns, smooth and relatively easy to fish. Out of it came three trout each of which would have taken an honourable place in the baskets which I used to carry home from this burn in my boyhood; but today, like all those before, they were returned to live and rise again, I hoped, some other day.

The stream had fallen as the day went on and now above the junction the burn was small and very clear. With my time now running short I fished on rapidly towards the road and the car, trying only a few of the bigger pools and spending some time in an attempt to hook a trout of some size which was rising in a deep narrow pool between two rock faces where for many years a sheep bridge crossed the stream. But he would have none of me, and reeling up my line I went back under the old ash trees to the road and the car. I had not kept an accurate account of the trout caught and returned but there had certainly been at least three dozen, probably rather more. As I took down my rod and removed my waders I reflected, perhaps with some nostalgic regret, on the pride with which in days now so long ago I would have counted and displayed my catch in the kitchen at Foswell where Annie the old cook would have shared my pleasure, even if the prospect of dealing with nearly forty small trout filled her with secret consternation.

So I went home with an empty basket but a happy heart. I do not doubt that had I used the old method of two small wet flies I would have caught nearly, if not quite, as many trout and possibly with less effort of eye, arm and wrist. Whether they would have been of equal quality I think more doubtful. I have always thought that on river and stream alike the better and more lively trout rise to the floating

rather than to the sunk fly. This may be a complete delusion, but as
I looked back on that May afternoon on the Pairney Burn I at least
felt sure that for me there can be few greater pleasures than to float
a fly on running water in beautiful surroundings and to watch the
rise of a trout.

CHAPTER 9

The sea pool of the River Awe

The pool lies near the river mouth close enough to the salt water of Loch Etive to feel the ebb and flow of the tide. When the tide is going out you may start fishing some two hours before low water and if you wish you can fish on until the tide has turned and has been flowing in for two hours. Then the salt water again comes into the pool filling it at length right up to the overhanging alders on the east bank and fishing is useless till hours later when the turn of the tide has emptied it and has made it again a sea-trout pool.

On the first day we fished the pool, low water was at 1 pm so about 11 am we arrived at the river mouth where the ferry would take us over to the east bank from which we must fish. A fresh west wind blew up Loch Etive and hummed in the telephone wires which here cross the loch at a great height in one huge span, while the waves meeting the outgoing tide and the current of the river where the loch narrows, made a tumble of white and broken water from which gusts blew the spray in little showers. A sheet of foam, caught in an eddy of the current, swung round and round breaking into little cakes lightly tinged with brown. At the river mouth and on the shores of the loch, sand and gravel wet from the falling tide glistened in the sun, and the fresh salt smell of drying seaweed was a joy to the senses.

Laden with waders and rods we made our way down to the water's edge picking our way among little pools where pink and yellow weed and hosts of tiny shells lay in the clear brackish water. Between the pools sea asters grew, like purple-blue daisies, scattered through the rich green of the salt grass. There was no sign of the ferryman on the far side of the river, but presently we saw him coming down to the shore through the great ash trees beside the ruins of the old inn used by drovers and other wayfarers in days long past, whose front of broken roughcast looks over the river mouth from frameless windows and gaping doors. He came for us in his rickety boat making a great detour upstream to defeat the strength of the river and outgoing tide which swept him down as he edged crabwise across the current to ground on the gravel near where we stood. In midstream two wild swans, unafraid of the old man and his boat, swam almost stationary against the current and as he passed close to them the cock bird continued his exploration of the river bed below, bringing to the surface in his beak a trail of green weed while his tail wagged vigorously in satisfaction. The ferryman told us that the birds had nested that spring in the marshy ground at the head of a backwater near the ferry, but a high spring tide had covered the nest and the eggs in it and they had not built again.

Landing on the east side of the ferry we made our way upstream through scattered alder seedlings which grow among the stones of the river bank in an undergrowth of bog-myrtle, heather and scabious. As we came in sight of the pool we could see that the tide was almost out of it, leaving between the water's edge and the thick alders on the bank a broad stretch of stony shore up which we stumbled with our loads till we had come about half way up the pool. Here in a sheltered corner under the alders we sat to put on waders and set up our rods.

Sheltered from the upstream wind it was warm, and as we sat under the alders a peacock butterfly, the first of several which we were to see by the pool, settled on the stones at our feet. It looked almost black as it sat poised with wings erect, but when it spread them to rest on the stone a rich velvet brown showed, edged with cream and broken near the point of the wing by the rainbow colours of the round peacock marking.

The main current of the river runs close to the far side of the pool opposite where we sat, flowing swiftly under a steep bank which rises to a pasture field and the whitewashed buildings of a farm. Very little of the pool is calm water and near the neck it is all broken and rapid, but between where we sat and the edge of the strong current was a belt of less rapid stream eddying deep and tempting. We had with us nothing larger than trout rods, 10 foot and 9½ foot, though the pool was much too wide for us to cover it with them. We had debated whether we should bring a 12 foot sea-trout rod, but had decided against it, preferring the ease and comfort of the light rods, despite the risk which we knew we ran. My brother fished the neck and the upper half of the pool while I waded in nearly opposite the spot where we had sat and fished from there down to the tail. Each of us used a 2X cast and small sea-trout flies. My piece of water produced only two finnock and half-hearted rises from a few others, and remembering a successful experiment on the same pool some years before, I waded ashore and set up a dry fly rod with a tapered cast and a fair sized March Brown tied with upright hackles which I picked from my box, largely because it seemed big enough to be clearly visible from a distance in the broken water. With the line greased I waded in near where a piece of smoother water on the edge of the main stream seemed to offer a chance for a dry fly. It was an immediate success. The larger fish indeed showed small interest, but the finnock and small sea-trout greeted the floating fly with joy and I had already caught three and lost several others when a shout from my brother made me look up to see him playing a heavy fish. It was soon evident that this was a salmon and a lively one at that, for it kept far out into the current and showed a tendency to go off downstream, a manoeuvre which the small rod battling against the weight of fish, line and river could not possibly prevent. But there were no obstacles immediately below us or indeed between us and the salt water, so the position was reasonably secure if the gut and the hold of the small hook were equal to the strain. The wild energy of the fish was its own undoing and presently after some anxious moments the odds ceased to be in favour of the salmon.

There can be few inveterate fishermen who tempt Providence so consistently as my brother and myself, and it was not surprising that on this, as on so many other occasions, we lacked the gaff which common prudence would have provided. Our nets were made for no more than sea-trout. The fish looked big and the outlook black; but once in the slack water near the edge the salmon proved to be much exhausted and after one unsuccessful effort on my part to net it, it obligingly swam into the net at the second attempt and, once its head and shoulders were in, the rest followed with surprising ease and we waded ashore carrying in triumph a short thick salmon of 7½lb. The pool was now much disturbed so we made for home, passing on our way the opening stages of a jumble sale in aid of local charities where the small sea-trout served a useful purpose, though in surroundings humiliating and incongruous to fish so recently come from the tidal water in all the pride of silver and blue.

Two days later we again fished the pool, but on that day the tide did not suit till 3 o'clock in the afternoon. During the summer months at the time of which I write the motor post-boat took the mail each morning 10 miles up to the head of Loch Etive, and we decided to go part of the way in her, being dropped off in our row boat to fish round the shore for the sea-trout which here at certain times of the year will rise to a fly quite readily in the brackish water near the mouths of the burns. The motor boat would pick us up again on her return trip in time for us to reach the pool at 3 o'clock. In Cadderlie Bay the motor boat was stopped; the row boat towed behind us was hauled alongside and we got into her with our rods and nets. Then we pushed off, and rowing in to the shore lay in the shelter of a rocky point while we put up the rods. Helped by a good breeze we drifted across the bay past the sandy mouth of the burn which here comes down the hill-side in a deep gully and runs the last few hundred yards to the loch through a tunnel of overhanging alders. The bay looked ideal, but we saw no sea-trout either in it or round the rocky point at its far end where the high tide makes an island of the extreme point of the promontory on which a single rowan tree and a great heap of stones mark the site of some old building. We drifted a little way up the loch towards Dall and then, as it seemed that the sea-trout had left that part of the loch on their way up towards the river at its head, we landed, disturbing a solitary oyster-catcher which went off along the loch side, its startled call dying gradually in the distance far down the shore. Slipping and stumbling across the wet seaweed left by the falling tide to the dry granite rocks of the shore we pushed our way up through a belt of bracken and on to a ledge of grass and heather which faced the loch from the shelter of a rocky knoll. Here we lunched, looking down the loch to the woods of Glen Liever and Glen Noe on the far shore where the hay stood in little ricks in the meadows below the shepherd's house, and across to the mouth of Glen Kinglass.

It was a day of soft grey sombre light. The mist hung heavy over-head hiding the tops of the higher hills and coming part of the way down the sides of Ben Treallachain and Ben Starav near the head of the loch. There was little distant view and only with difficulty could we make out the saddle between the Buchaille Etives at the head of the Glen 12 miles away. Even the nearby corrie was partially hidden in thick haze and dark shadow across which trailed rags and wisps of mist from the belt of cloud hanging on the hillside close above; but immediately behind us on the hillside colours, shapes and outlines took on in that dark light a rare depth and solidity. A great piece of flat ground covered with bog myrtle stretched to the foot of the hill. Then the ground rose steeply through hillocks of rank grass and brac-ken patches to rocky outcrops and short heather with stunted alder and birches in the corrie down which runs the Cadderlie Burn. It seemed that every shade of green was there. The soft green of the bog-myrtle, the brighter green of the rank grass, the dark shiny green of the bracken patches and the blue-green of the high slopes changing to olive and then to brown as the eye lifted to the short heather of the high slopes; till just under the mist was intense shadow deepening to black where the hillside disappeared into the hanging clouds. The whole made a striking picture—vivid, imminent and almost menacing.

We lay for long above the shore while the familiar detail of bracken and bog-myrtle, granite gravel and bell-heather recalled other days on hill and river at Glen Etive stretching back almost to the earliest limits of childhood's memory. We watched the wooded point at Barrs beyond which showed on the far shore the water-scarred slopes of Ben Starav and when the launch appeared, a white speck round the point, we pushed off the boat and rowed out into the loch where we lay waiting for her, rolling and pitching gently in the fresh west wind. Tied again to the stern of the launch our boat strained at the end of the tow rope, its nose in the air and its stern sunk low in a jumble of white water, while we lay on the upper deck of the launch facing into the cold steady push of the wind as the boat butted her way down the loch. Behind us the hills of Glen Etive and the dark fir woods of Craigdubh receded and dimmed to our view as they had done so often in years long past, to rise again more clearly before the eye of memory.

Coming ashore from the launch we crossed again by the ferry at the river mouth. A fresh breeze blew upstream as we reached our sheltered corner under the alders by the sea pool. Subdued sunlight breaking partially through the cloud gave a touch of brown to the deep eddies on the edge of the stream and sparkled on the broken water at the neck of the pool. This time we pinned our faith entirely to the dry fly and to increase its chances I tied a second fly on the cast where, had one been using wet fly, the bob fly would have hung. It is a device which for some reason I had only lately started to use, but one which I believe in proper conditions to be highly effective. Certainly it proved so as we used it on the tidal pool and as on the previous day the finnock greeted the floating flies like old friends. These fish seem the very embodiment of life, movement and gaiety. If there is such a thing as a really happy fish, it must surely be the finnock. Entering the fresh water in all the joy and pride of youth, filled with the energy stored up during the preceding months of good living in salt water, the finnock suffers little from the preoccupation and responsibility of its larger relations. The bigger fish are in the fresh water for a set purpose bound on a long and dangerous journey from which so many of them do not return; but the finnock is still only on the threshold. It flirts with life, often playing a fascinating game of tip and run between the fresh water and the salt—between the serious business of life and the playground—venturing only a little way up the river and ready to flash down through the lower pools and out again to the tidal water.

That day on the tidal pool the finnock showed all the characteristics which put them in the very front rank of sporting fish. Some took the fly with a quick splashing rush, others with a deliberate head and tail rise, and some behaved as I have seen trout behave on a chalk stream during the first rapture of the mayfly season, shooting as much as two feet out of the water, though whether they caught the fly on the upward rush or as they came down I could not be sure. Some in their eagerness missed the fly, but by such a narrow margin that when we struck, the hook caught them in the body and when this happened they shot off into the stream with a strength which a fish hooked in the mouth could never equal.

One of the main difficulties of this type of fishing is to keep the fly constantly in view. In the comparatively calm waters of a chalk stream this is a matter of little difficulty, but to see a small dry fly at the end of ten yards of line as it dances and tosses on the surface of a strong current where the eye is confused by the dappled and changing lights and reflections from a hundred eddies is a different matter. But it must be done if one is to gain that added quickness in striking which means so much. Soon the eye acquires a surprising skill and acuteness aided by an instinctive knowledge of where the fly should be, so that even if you fail to see it land, your eye will often pick it up as it floats down past you; and there is something fascinating in that little speck of brown seen through the silver reflections, sitting on its hackles on the top of the current and dancing down gaily and fearlessly as if to challenge all comers. Here it must be admitted that the use of two dry flies on the cast tends to confuse the issue, for the eye and attention may be focused on one while the rise comes to the other; but the two flies are seldom floating far apart and the eye which sees the one will seldom fail to be aware of a rise to the other. The method is, of course, totally unsuitable where, as on a chalk stream, one is fishing for a particular trout, but where, as so often on northern streams, the fisherman is casting over rough swift water for unseen trout the balance of advantage lies often, I believe, on the side of using two flies.

Gradually we fished our way up the pool, casting sometimes in the calm water on the near side of the current, sometimes to the edge of the broken water and occasionally far out into the stream where the fly tossed and tumbled, a very little thing in the grip of the great river; and everywhere were the finnock, even in the very neck of the pool. Here in the thin rapid stream the water foamed and splashed round our waders. The sound of rushing water filled the hearing, while the eye was dazzled and bewitched by the sight of the hurrying river, sparkling in the sun and whipped by the upstream breeze. Far above the sea pool was the calm water of a salmon pool, but between lay a long shallow, a stretch of swift glittering water. So we fished in a foreground of dancing eddies of silver and brown with the glittering shallow beyond; and farther still, though the eye could not often lift to it from the water, was the feathery green of the tall larches of the Inverawe woods backed by the great shoulder of Cruachan.

But now the tide had turned and was creeping up the river, damming back the fresh water and smothering the current of the pool. The water level had crept nearer the line of the alders on the bank and the best of the fishing was over for that day. We waded ashore, took down our rods and collected up and down the bank where we had laid them twenty-two sea-trout, varying from some finnock of rather more than $\frac{1}{2}$lb to a number of adult sea-trout of 1lb and over. So we went home, leaving the pool and the finnock, some perhaps to move down again to the salt water of the river mouth where the swans fish and the ferry boat crosses, others to move up, newcomers, to where the streams and eddies would reflect in silver the sunlight of another day.

CHAPTER 10

A July day in Argyll

Early one morning in the first days of July I stood on a terrace over-looking a sea-loch on the west coast of Scotland. At my feet the ground fell steeply to the water's edge 200 feet below, hazel and rowan, birch and stunted oak trees clothing the steep slope. They grew from a tangle of deep bracken, ferns and rhododendrons—a thick luxuriance of green undergrowth still wet with the morning dew, from which came up to me where I stood the fresh sweet scents which belong to the sea-board of Argyll. Directly below me and divided from the mainland by a narrow strip of quiet water lay a low green island, in shape so fantastic as to suggest a piece of a jig-saw puzzle. From every side little bays ran deeply in towards the heart of the island, as if Nature had designed them as safe harbours where little boats could find shelter from every wind. But that morning not a breath of wind ruffled the surface of the loch round the island and the only ripples came from the head of one tiny bay where a pair of mergansers moved among the patches of seaweed floating on the half tide. On the island itself the few sheep which graze there moved through wet grass growing thickly among the scattered stones of some ancient ruined building, while above them and over the whole island hovered and wheeled the terns and sea-gulls whose crying had not ceased all through the twilight of the short summer night. Far down the loch I could trace from the height of the terrace the eddies of current from the incoming tide. Here and there were little patches of ripple which might later spread and unite into a steady breeze over the whole loch's surface, but seemed more likely to die away and reappear elsewhere, fickle and elusive.

Beyond the westward bend of the loch, the clouds hung half way down the slope of the hillside, and far out to the west the rising bulk of Ben More in Mull was no more than a dim outline soon lost as it rose into the mist and heavy cloud above. The soft still dampness of the air and the little rags of mist hanging from dark threatening clouds which lay low above the olive green of the wooded hills all spoke of the south wind, and looking up it seemed that the almost motionless clouds were drifting very slowly northward over the low wooded skyline beyond which lay Loch Avich and Loch Awe. So when later that morning I set out to fish the lochs which lie in the hills, I knew that I must be prepared for a day of flat calm or at best one of short unsteady puffs of breeze, for a long succession of summers and autumns in the west has taught that the south wind seldom brings other than days of indeterminate weather; days when Nature threatens terrible things of rain and thunder which seldom come in the end to more than drizzle and light showers; days of soft colour and soft air, unsuited to hard walking, but quiet and restful to the eyes and senses. I knew, too, that little rain had fallen during the last few weeks; that the sea-trout which later enter the lochs for which I was bound could have had no chance to run up from the salt water and that I could hope for nothing but small brown trout. So it was with no exaggerated hopes or expectations that I started off.

The way to the lochs follows for most of its length a grass-grown cart track which bends and turns among the endless little hills typical of south Argyll, some no more than knolls covered with rank heather and stunted willow, but others rising to the dignity of hillocks covered with hazel and small oak trees whose long mossy branches hang low over slopes blue in spring with wild hyacinths and now covered with beds of bracken. On all sides was rich and luxuriant growth and every shade of green in tree and bush, in bracken and bog-myrtle and in the rank grass between the tall heads of which spiders had stretched their webs and woven their little nests, a gossamer tracery silvered over with a myriad of tiny beads of moisture. On my left the ground rose slowly to the south showing a wide hillside dotted with countless little hollows and wooded hillocks like those through which I was passing, and most of which will lie from year's end to year's end disturbed only by blackgame, woodcock and roe deer. Beyond the sky-line lay, I knew, mile upon mile of such ground rising gradually to the far ridge and then falling to the shores of Loch Awe, many miles to the south. I found myself wondering at the thought of the vast tracts of the earth's surface where, as on this little stretch of Argyllshire hillside, a wealth of colour and growth and natural beauty ebbs and flows undisturbed and almost unseen through the endless cycles of the passing seasons.

Presently a thin drizzle came on, but so fine were the drops and so lightly did they fall that I seemed to be moving through a mist of moisture suspended in the warm air. Despite the fine rain and the heavy atmosphere, it seemed that the sun might at any moment break through. The heat was oppressive and I was not sorry when the path dipped occasionally to cross little streams running under the cool shade of low-hanging hazels. The dry weather had shrunk the burns till only small trickles flowed in beds of dry stones stained to a dark brown from the peat water which covers them when the burns are full. Wild iris grew tall along the edges, and in the shallows at the tails of the biggest pools tiny trout darted upstream to the deeper water. These little trout, darting for cover in the smallest of peaty trickles in Argyllshire, are such a familiar sight that I have come to think that such streams can support nothing bigger and that perhaps these tiny fish are in fact the full grown adult inhabitants of the little brown hazel-shaded pools in which they live.

An hour's walk brought me to a deserted croft which stands at the edge of open meadow ground stretching to the loch in the hollow below. As I passed between the empty steading and the silent cottage, an oyster-catcher flew up to perch on the top of a harled chimney stalk from which it sent startled and indignant cries echoing far over the broad meadow land. The sound shattered a silence which may have lain over that place for days before my coming, and as I made my way through the rushes and rich thick grass of the meadow, I felt an intruder and a disturber of the peace. The shrill warning of the oyster-catcher and my own passage through the meadow had alarmed the sand-pipers and redshanks, and my way to the loch was marked by a running accompaniment of their calls as each bird in turn circled crying over my head till I had passed the dry ditch or the deep tuft where her young ones crouched. Presently the path led to a rough bridge of railway sleepers over a deep slow stream. Here I crossed, climbing with some difficulty through a barricade of old birch poles and rusty barbed wire which the crofters on either side of the stream had put up to prevent their beasts from straying. In the middle of the bridge I stood for a moment looking over into the deep black water which moved so slowly that only from the very slight bend of the underwater weeds could one tell that it flowed westward from the invisible loch on my right into the one for which I was making. Along the far side of the stream I turned through soft ground and bog-myrtle and in a few hundred yards came to the little bay near the end of the loch where the boat is moored.

Above the bay is a small bracken-covered hillock and this I climbed to sit on the dry bell-heather of the top looking down and out over the loch's surface. All the fisherman's doubts in the early morning seemed justified, for beyond the broad belt of reeds which stretched below me with hardly a rustle in the still air, the loch lay black and smooth, an ebony expanse with a polished surface. Far out in the centre the smoothness was broken by the occasional ring of a rising trout, and near at hand small ripples spread outwards from the edge of the water-lilies where a water-hen was moving. The thin drizzle had cleared away as the sun broke partially through the heavy clouds and for a time I sat there watching and waiting and at last half asleep. After a time the soft rustle of the reeds below roused me to the knowledge that a slight breeze was coming across the loch from the southwest corner, rippling the surface and drifting before it a thin film of drizzling rain. Making my way down to the water's edge I put up my rod and pushing off in the boat made my way slowly through the tall reeds and finally over the glistening leaves of the water-lilies towards the open water. The reeds catching the breeze seemed like a forest of lances with fluttering pennants on which the water splashed from the oars lay in silver dust and crystal beads scattered over the green. As I neared their edge where the deep water starts I felt again something of the reluctance which as a boy I had always felt when pushing out on to the black surface of the loch. It was partly a hesitation to disturb its quietness, but partly, I knew, a childish fear of finding myself alone out on the black surface of the water, isolated and divided from the shore by the broad thick belts of reeds which ring the loch on every side. I had to admit to a sense of comfort and companionship as I saw at a little distance the blue smoke from a croft rising straight in the still air from behind a hillock, and on the hillside beyond, the crofter and his boy working on their little patch of turnips.

For the next two hours I fished leisurely round the edge of the water-lilies, letting the boat drift before any breeze which came. Plenty of very small trout were rising, but they were in that most annoying of all moods when they pluck the fly under water, making off hurriedly and unscathed as if engaged in a great game of tip and run. Such a mood in the trout produces in the fisherman a corresponding mood of exasperation and impatience. He takes to striking wildly, quickly and seldom with effect, except on occasions when a very small trout, less circumspect than the rest, has swallowed the fly and is jerked from the water over the fisherman's shoulder into the water behind.

Landing for lunch and tying the rope of the boat round an old root of bog-myrtle, I climbed the hillside and sat again on the heather of its top. Then finding a comfortable sloping bank for my back, I lay watching the heavy clouds move slowly above me as I drifted from contemplation, through drowsiness, into sleep. When I woke, a slight breeze was again striking the loch from the south-west, and rowing round to the west end I drifted before it till it gradually died away leaving the boat lying motionless in the still and smooth water. At one corner of the loch's west end the water narrows and the reeds close in round a lane of water which runs far back among the scrub birch and bog-myrtle of the surrounding bog and leads eventually to the deep peaty burn which drains the loch and winds through bog-land and meadow to the distant sea-loch. A belt of water-lilies divides the main loch from this narrow strip of water on which I could see the light breeze still striking. Turning the boat I rowed over to that corner and pushing through the belt of water-lilies presently found myself floating clear of them in the narrow water. The breeze seen from a distance proved little more than a will-o'-the-wisp and almost before I had got the boat into position to drift, it died away leaving the boat once more floating motionless on the smooth black surface. This time I had no hope of finding a ripple elsewhere, so continued casting lazily and mechanically and without any hope of success. Suddenly a great wave started to form in the still water beyond my tail fly, and growing quickly it engulfed the fly and died away while a heavy weight came on the rod and line. In the short interval between the appearance of the wave and the coming of the weight on the line, there had been time to reflect that this was early July when the big sea-trout begin to run but to call to mind also the drought of the last six weeks during which it seemed impossible that any fish had been able to enter the loch from the salt water. So it was that when I struck the fish and felt its great weight on my small rod, I had reached no conclusion but only a state of complete doubt and some incredulity.

One big fish hooked in a loch is apt to play much like another and the only unusual circumstances which can be claimed for the fight on which I now became engaged were the absence of a net, and the fact that I was alone in a boat surrounded on three sides by beds of reed and water-lilies, the nearest only a few feet away. Had the fish made even reasonably good use of the opportunities which beckoned at every turn, I have no doubt that I should have lost fish and cast in a very short time; but this fish preferred to pursue a sullen and unenterprising course round and round the boat, a proceeding enlivened only by the fact that periodically the boat drifted in to one or other of the nearby beds of water-lilies from which I had to move it out as best I could with one oar while playing the fish with the other hand. Gradually the fish came nearer the surface and as I shortened the line I realised more and more acutely the difficulties facing me owing to the lack of a net. Presently I began to catch glimpses of the fish far down in the peaty water, and of an unhappy small trout which having swallowed the dropper during the fight had become the unwilling ally and close companion of the big fish whose great length as it came gradually nearer to the surface I could now see. Seldom have I seen a fish in fresh water less prepossessing in appearance and had it been in the sea I should, without hesitation, have put it down as a great dog-fish. The lanky appearance and the white on its under-side as it turned, confirmed my earlier suspicions that late in the season as it was I had hooked a great kelt sea-trout, a fish which had come up into the loch on its way to the spawning grounds in the hill burns the previous autumn, but which by some mischance had lingered on the return journey till the inclination and even perhaps the ability to go back to salt water had left it. Its condition explained its lack of enterprise when hooked and to that alone was it due that some little time later, having first freed the small trout, I was able to get my hand round the narrow part of the tail of the big fish and drag over the boat's side a sea-trout which, had it been in condition must have weighed a good 5lb. A few seconds later it was back in the water, and still holding it by the tail I pointed its head towards the entrance to the burn and pushed it away with the hope that it would somehow make its way down to the salt water and that it might be given to me on some other day to encounter it again after it had recovered its full strength and condition.

Late in the evening of that same day I stood beside a great pool on the river Awe under the shadow of Cruachan. The river was running low after the long drought, but even so the surface of the upper half of the pool was, at the time of which I write, alive with great eddies formed by the suck of the strong rush of the stream among the big boulders beneath the surface. Below, the eddies died gradually away as the river broadened out into the smoother expanse of the wide pool. Here, far out in the quieter water, the head and shoulders of great fish would now and then break the surface with the effortless movement of the porpoise whose size they seemed to rival. Leaving one member of the party to fish the pool, we made our way upstream. Soon after the river leaves Loch Awe, it flows in a broad swift stream, shallow on the near side, but deepening gradually to the far bank, and here we stopped. My companion, starting from the neck of the pool, fished the stream with a 14 foot rod and a small salmon fly, and waiting till he had fished down some little distance, I waded in behind him at the top of the rough water to try with a trout rod for the brown trout which earlier in the week we had found rising along the edges of the stream. As I made my way out through the shallow water, I stopped to look about me in the failing light. The coming of evening had brought no change to the dark heavy clouds and the warm still air of the day. The mist hung low and motionless on the sides of Cruachan whose rocky slopes disappearing upwards into the gloom gave an impression of wild and savage immensity. Behind me in the narrowing pass the deep waters of the Pass of Brander lay still and black. Immediately below me the river widened out into the broad stream at the tail of which it broke in the first of a series of rough white rapids which extend far downstream. Their sound, enclosed by the heavy clouds hanging so close above and the steep hills on either side seemed dulled in pitch but magnified in volume adding if possible to the wildness of the scene. With a vivid, but not unpleasant, sense of my surroundings, I started casting out into the broken water which lay along the edge of the fast current of the main stream.

For the first few yards I saw and felt nothing, but presently I came to a part where the shallow water of the neck begins to deepen and here my fly was seized by some heavy fish. At first it showed little enterprise, remaining in the shallow water and leading me to the conclusion that I had hooked merely a large trout, but presently it made out into the current and set off downstream with an unhurried deliberation which left me in no doubt of its size and strength and set me shouting to my companion now fishing well down the pool. The fight which followed was in marked contrast to the dull sullen struggle of the afternoon, the only point of similarity lying in the inadequacy of the rod on each occasion for the work it was called on to do. But now I had a companion with a net and it was thanks to them that half an hour later we waded ashore taking with us a fresh-run sea-trout of 5¾lb, and again a very small trout which had swallowed the dropper and was now quite exhausted by its unwilling participation in the fight.

It pleased me to imagine that the wishes which had followed the old sea-trout as it swam off tired but unhurt earlier in the day had been fulfilled beyond all my expectations and that by some magic spell of the Good Fairies it had been given to me, a few miles away, to meet again and catch that same sea-trout now fat and strong from the rich feeding of the open sea. Even the small trout had not been forgotten.

CHAPTER 11

A Somerset trout stream

The little stream rises on the slopes of the Mendips and flows eastwards for a few miles to join the Avon below the small town of Frome near the borders of Somerset and Wiltshire. In its lower reaches it is a slow deep stream and I believe that in the autumn sea-trout and a few salmon make their way up it from the Bristol Channel; but the only part I ever knew was a very short stretch where a quiet by-road from Radstock to Frome dips steeply to cross the stream at the lovely village of Mells.

My first memory of Mells and its stream dates back to the early 1920s when we spent three happy weeks living in a farmhouse between Mells and Stratton-on-the-Fosse working for university exams. My chief recollection of that time is that in the early morning, while the dew was still on the grass, we used to gather great baskets of mushrooms which grew abundantly in the small rich pasture fields round the farm; but sometimes we helped with the hay harvest and though we had no rods with us we explored the stream near Mells and the two artificial lakes which lie just upstream from the village. I suppose we also found time to do some of the reading for which we had come. The memory of that is less clear, but the exams were successfully passed, so presumably this part of our programme was not entirely neglected.

There are two lakes on the stream at Mells, the upper one lying in open park land and the lower deep-set among close surrounding woods. Between the two is a weir where the water passes over a considerable fall to form a deep pool, before it flows on to widen out into the lower lake. Several years passed during which we saw no more of the place, but then we came again, this time with rods and an invitation to fish. The numbers of the trout which we had seen on our earlier visit had, it seemed, in the interval grown greater rather than less and from their behaviour we judged that they had not been much fished for. The weir between the lakes proved the most productive and in many ways the most attractive spot. Here there was for a short distance enough current to work a wet fly cast and no doubt the freshness of the moving water in contrast with the stillness of the sheltered lake below accounted for the congregation of trout at this point. I cannot now recall how many we caught. The number was certainly considerable and though I do not think we caught any of outstanding size, the average weight was not far short of 1lb.

Our success was by no means confined to the pool below the weir; on the lower lake which proved the more productive of the two, we caught many from the bank. Here our efforts were much restricted by the fact that there was no boat available which would float. The soft edges prevented wading, while trees close to the water's edge and bushes overhanging the banks made casting difficult. Very many of the trout which cruised and fed in the lower lake kept far out and were quite out of reach; but from time to time and especially towards evening, they came closer and if the flies were put anywhere near a rising fish and moved very slowly in the still water they were usually taken. Only at one point could a long cast be safely made. A little way below the weir a water-logged punt was moored. It was entirely unseaworthy, but by climbing cautiously into it and casting in some peril from near the sunken stern, it was possible to reach trout which from the bank were quite beyond reach. A few casts from this vantage point soon disturbed the water, but after an interval the trout resumed their feeding and this point we found most productive.

It cannot be said that these fish showed much enterprise when they were hooked. Only below the weir in the running water were they at all lively. For the rest they seemed to rely mainly on their weight and few of them when hooked caused us much anxiety or excitement. At the foot of the lower lake the water passed over a smaller fall into the stream which disappeared into a green jungle of bushes and trees. Here at the outlet lived some more enterprising trout and as they fed mainly on insects which dropped off the bushes growing on the bank beside the outlet, we had some excitement and not a few disasters.

On our second visit we explored the stream below. Here were brisk shallow runs and some good pools with deep parts under the branches of overhanging trees, but now in the last days of June with the growth of weed and leaf and waterside herbage almost at its height, our way was not made easy. The use of a dry fly seemed out of the question in this overgrown spot and the best we could do was to drift a wet fly cast downstream in some of the opener places and hope for the best as it passed under the branches into the pools below. By this method we managed with some loss of flies and temper to catch a few, but the results were out of all proportion to the labour and risk, and we soon abandoned the stream in the knowledge that though it was full of trout the easier and larger, if not the better, fish were in the lakes.

The lakes at Mells were indirectly the occasion of my first casting a fly on the Test, and here I must make a belated apology to those who at that time owned the fishing on the piece of water where it occurred. My brother and a friend and I had been fishing the Mells lakes one day in early July and as I had to catch a very late train from London to Scotland we left Mells by car in the late afternoon. Our road led us by Warminster and Amesbury. The air was cool after the heat of the day and the light of early evening was on the Downs. We dined at a small inn beyond Andover, and later took the main road for London which crosses the Test some way below Whitchurch. At that point the Test, if my memory serves, flows in three sections, the middle one a deep narrow stream carrying a large part of the river. Time was not yet pressing and as we reached the bridge we stopped to see if the evening rise had yet started. Downstream the river widened out into a broad pool at the tail of which trout were already feeding. Upstream was deep narrow water. Here were no signs of trout, but flies were beginning to come down and as we watched a good trout started to feed in the centre of the current only a few yards above the bridge. We watched him, fascinated and covetous for a few minutes as he continued to eat each fly which came to him. How the unholy thought came to us and who first gave heed to it I do not know; but come it did, while we looked at one another 'with a wild surmise', silent as Cortez and his men in Darien. Having once started us down the primrose path, the Tempter was not slow to show us the way and the means. Evening was approaching. No one was within sight. Our rods and tackle were ready to hand in the boot of the car, while only a few cars were passing along the road. The sight of the trout feeding steadily on swept aside all scruple, and in that instant we were fairly launched on a career of crime. My brother pulled three grasses of uneven length from the side of the road and held them for my friend and me to draw, the final holder of the longest grass to be the main actor in the coming drama. I guessed correctly and soon my rod was up with the line threaded and a cast attached. I cannot remember what fly I used but I seem to recall that it was a Ginger Quill. At this point several cars passed us on the road. Mercifully none of them stopped to look at the river and meantime we had to appear to be idly enjoying Nature while the rod lay flat on the road hidden by the car. Soon there came a pause in the traffic and the curtain went up. In the excitement my aim was worse than usual and the first two casts went astray but not sufficiently so to put the trout down. Then came a car and I had hastily to lay the rod on the road, the cast and fly fending for themselves. The car passed; the line, cast and fly were recovered intact and a hurried cast put the Ginger Quill where it ought to be. The trout, a fish of some 2lb, rose and was firmly hooked. He went upstream and then turned down as if to pass through the bridge below us. Another car came in sight and as I could no longer use the rod it had to be hastily laid down while I tried surreptitiously to keep the line tight by hand. When the car had passed we found, not surprisingly, that the trout had profited by the interlude to bury himself in a weed bed below the bridge. We could not move him from where we stood and as more cars were approaching and time was now short, we had to pull hard on the line. Luckily the hold gave way, so that we recovered line, cast and fly which was more than we deserved or expected. As we hurriedly took down the rod and repacked it in the boot of the car, we reflected that at least we had scored a moral victory over that trout—but perhaps looking back on it all 'moral' is not the right word after all! I need only add that I caught the train for Scotland by a very narrow margin.

During the war and for the first year or two immediately after it, I was little at Mells, but then my visits became more frequent and my most recent fishing there was in the summer of 1957. The lakes were no longer available and it was only in the stream that I could fish. I had spent a morning in May of that year in renewing my acquaintance with the short stretch just above the village and had found it still full of trout. At that time the stream was full and clear and though it was, as before, much overgrown, the spring growth had not yet made it impossible to fish and had I then had a rod with me something might have been done. I came to Mells again in the third week in June taking with me this time a three-piece 8 foot rod belonging to my wife, which, among other merits, fits into a short aluminium case for travelling.

The clock of Mells church had just struck eleven as I crossed the main road which runs through the village and made for the river. Tarquin, a large Gordon Setter belonging to my hostess, had come to expect from me a walk as a matter of right and I took him with me hoping, with little confidence, that I could impress on him that this was a rather special kind of walk, calling for special behaviour. It was a lovely summer's morning and the cottage gardens were gay with Sweet William and pinks, hollyhocks and Canterbury Bells and all the good old-fashioned flowers to which, thanks be to them, cottage gardeners remain ever faithful. Valerian in all shades of pink and red bent over the lane from limestone banks and cottage walls, as Tarquin and I walked to the lower end of the meadow where the stream enters the village. The volume of water had dwindled sadly since early May, while the growth of leaf and grass and every growing thing beside the stream had gone far to make for it a green tunnel. Up through the meadow Tarquin and I made our way stopping here and there to peer through the foliage. Trout were rising in the stiller water but nowhere was there the least possibility of casting a fly. We came at last to a short open stretch below a foot bridge where trout were rising. The far bank was free from trees and from it I saw that I could cast. We crossed the footbridge cautiously, my hand through Tarquin's collar and, making a detour, came to the lower end of the open stretch at a point within easy casting distance of a spot where the stream ran between weed beds in a deep narrow channel. In the waist-high growth of grass and reeds beside the stream was a fair sprinkling of nettles and thistles, and obeying that instinct which so quickly warns dogs of their presence, Tarquin decided to my relief to stay on the foot-path well back from the water. Now at last there seemed some chance of success; but I had reckoned without Tarquin's sense of tactics and love of the water, for making a detour upstream he plunged into the river above me and came bounding down the centre of the stream in a storm of spray and exuberance—and that was the end of that.

Above the footbridge, cottage gardens and a further stretch of trees made fishing impossible but beyond them we came to another meadow, already cut for hay, which promised better things. The trees beside the river were slightly thinner. The old dog, too, was feeling the heat, and this—if not my straight words to him about the bathing episode—made him more ready to lie in the shade and leave me in some peace to what he clearly regarded as my inscrutable devices. The hay-cutters' activities had stopped a little short of the river bank, tall grasses thus adding to the hazards of the trees. In a shallow stream a trout rose and an underhand cast of, as I thought, great cunning ended in the disaster which it no doubt deserved, and the next ten minutes were spent in painfully disentangling fly and nylon from a clump of cow parsley, the intricacy of whose stems, foliage and bloom seemed designed for this very occasion.

We came at last to the top of the meadow. Here the stream passed under a side road beyond which I could not go. Immediately below the bridge was a promising piece of shallow water, but the bank was much overgrown with grass and nettles while an orchard just behind made casting, it seemed, impossible, and after a short survey I decided that nothing more could be done.

Before starting home Tarquin and I stood for a few minutes on the bridge looking downstream on the shallow water and beyond to a tempting pool hopelessly overhung by trees. In the shallow water a good trout was lying obviously on the look-out for flies, and as I watched he rose. From where I stood leaning on the stone parapet, it seemed just possible that a fly could, after all, be cast over him from below. So Tarquin and I made a hurried detour and came upstream to within casting distance. The prospects were far from rosy, but here was a good trout feeding in what seemed at least a possible position. After a short period of trial and error during which a young plum tree in the orchard suffered minor damage, my Iron Blue floated over the trout to be entirely ignored. Twice more it passed close to him and now it seemed clear that I was tempting Providence to no purpose; but in my fly box was a very tiny Greenwell's Glory, ooo in size, tied with a hackle in place of a wing. The first cast was beyond the trout and when at the second the fly passed exactly over him, I felt sure he had seen the gut at the first attempt and would have none of me. The third and final cast was slightly short, the fly passing about a foot to his right and floating past him. He made no move, but suddenly, as a naturally aggressive batsman after a long period of prudent restraint throws caution to the winds and chases a ball out on the off-side, he turned downstream in pursuit; and in a moment I had him in the slips.

A good trout hooked in very shallow water acquires a wonderful degree of speed and agility. With light tackle one dare not hold him tight and I had no net. My trout made for the far side where trailing branches spelt danger. The Gods were with me, the branches were avoided and a dash downstream where I could not have followed was foiled by the shallowness of the water. After further perilous excursions to the far bank the trout made upstream, and after an anxious moment came to rest half stranded against a piece of driftwood on the near side. From here I dared not dislodge him and there was no option but to wade upstream to where he lay. Now Tarquin lent a hand determined to show that he was as good in water as on land. Luckily his well-meant efforts were directed away from the danger point. As I neared the trout it floundered off the shingle and was again completely water-borne; but now it was much exhausted and with Tarquin at length back on dry land I was able at the third attempt to get the trout firmly into my hand and to regain the bank wet and stung with nettles on face and hands, but at last triumphant. The trout was rather less than $\frac{3}{4}$lb but as he lay on the grass I felt little doubt that his capture had given me far more satisfaction than many a fish of much greater weight caught in more orthodox and easier circumstances. Tarquin's reaction was striking. He paid me the compliment of showing the greatest interest in the trout and clearly indicated by his behaviour, or so it seemed, that I had now satisfactorily solved for him what had hitherto been an intriguing but unexplained mystery, and that in future he would be a model of fishing companions.

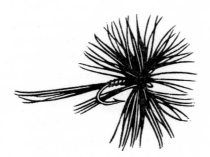

CHAPTER 12

Trout fishing in South Africa

On a misty morning towards the end of November 1963 we left the Thames on board one of the Union Castle liners bound for Durban on the south-east coast of Africa. The object of our journey was mainly to gain some weeks of freedom from the work and worries attached to an office, a farm and an estate; but we hoped in addition to get some trout fishing in South Africa, and accordingly our luggage included two light trout rods with appropriate reels and flies. The journey was uneventful, peaceful and increasingly warm, and we arrived in Durban at the very end of the year. The end of December is not a very suitable time to visit Durban or indeed almost any part of the Union. The South African summer is then at its height. The days are hot and, at least on the east coast, extremely humid, with thunderstorms and torrential rain at frequent intervals, and particularly in the evenings.

After nearly two weeks spent in or near Durban we set off by car for Himeville which lies about 130 miles inland close to the Drakensberg Mountains, one of the main objectives of our Natal visit. After climbing through the hills which lie immediately behind Durban the road to the mountains passes through rolling and well-cultivated land to the fine town of Pietermaritzburg, the administrative capital of Natal. Inland from Pietermaritzburg the road climbs very steeply and from this point on to Himeville one crosses ridge after ridge of increasingly high and rocky hills, occasionally dropping down into steep-sided valleys, but gaining height steadily.

The thunderstorms which we had had in Durban had been more violent in the hills, and as we came down the steep winding road into the deep valley of the Umkumaas River we could see that the river was running full and red, boding ill for our fishing. In this lies a major problem, not for the fisherman only but even more for the farmer and the administrator. For many of these rivers have their source at the heads of glens in the Drakensberg Mountains where several inches of rain may fall in an hour, and this may in the wet season be repeated day after day. When the streams leave the high hills they pass through an area of more rolling country where the hillsides, though still steep, grow good grass and in places fair crops of maize. The rich top soil, however, is relatively thin, overlaying what in Scotland we would call a 'pan' of much harder clay or even rock. Here over-grazing quickly eats through the grass and turf, the threadbare surface covering is no longer able to hold the loose soil against the action of rain which washes it down wholesale into the swollen rivers. Careless cultivation has the same effect, for unless the plough is driven along the hillside the furrows act as so many channels for erosion. Much is being attempted and something is being achieved to check this process by help and advice on contour ploughing and control of grazing, but, especially in the native reserves, there appears to be much apathy and improvidence and day by day in the wet season thousands of tons of rich African soil go on their way down to the Indian Ocean. The valley of the Umkumaas River provided a sad object lesson. The river was red with earth, and as we climbed from the valley on the far side we passed through large tracts of hard red clay from which all vestiges of life or growth had been washed away.

The tiny village of Himeville lies at an altitude of rather over 5,000 feet in a wide grassy plateau. This is rolling country, mainly pastoral, but broken here and there by patches of cultivation and with frequent shelter belts or larger plantations of pine and blue gum trees. To the north the rolling grassy hills rise gradually to higher and more rocky hills, but still grassy almost to the top, and behind these again rise the sharp peaks and jagged ridges of the main Drakensberg range, the final peaks 20 to 30 miles distant and 9,000 to 10,000 feet in height. To east, west and south are fold on fold of grassy hills, rising to higher and more distant ridges, which, with the Drakensberg, form the rim of this wide green basin. So, wherever one looks, the eye travels over rolling uplands to hills and still more hills. Dotted over this rolling country are clumps of fine pine, cedar and blue gum trees surrounding the white homesteads and outbuildings of the farms. Some of these farms are small by Natal standards, extending to only a few hundred acres. Many are several thousand acres in extent and some are even more. The names of very many of these farms recall the origin of their past or present owners and the close connections with England, Scotland and Ireland which is perhaps even more marked in Natal than in other parts of South Africa. The farms of Warwick, Epsom, Selborne and Abingdon, of Lammermoor, Gowrie and Chevy Chase lie on the lower ground. Nearer the hills are Killiecrankie and Seaforth, Cluny and Glenlyon, while far up the glens directly under the main Drakensberg ridge are Glengarry and Craig Dhu, Argyll and Lochiel. The islands, too, are recalled by the names of Islay, Stornoway and Stromness, and towards the end of our time in Himeville we often fished on water adjoining the farm of Dublin, with Glengariff and Dunraven not far off.

The great flood on the Umkumaas River which we had seen on our way from Durban had confirmed our fears that most of the rivers in the Himeville area would be out of order for fishing at least for several days. However, we had come to Himeville principally to fish and were determined to make the best of it, if only to be able to compare Natal fishing and Natal rivers with conditions at home. The village of Underberg, 4 miles from Himeville is the centre of the excellent Underberg/Himeville Fishing Club, and here in a thatched rondavel decorated with plaster casts of huge rainbow trout and pictures of English trout streams I became a temporary member of the

Club. Many of the Club members are local farmers and land-owners with whom the Club has arranged leases or other working arrangements and altogether it controls, I believe, about a hundred miles of very varied water on at least three main river systems, spread over a wide area which it carefully preserves and stocks. These river systems are fed by many streams coming down from Drakensberg; and in this lay the salvation of our fishing prospects. For the violent rain-storms which at this time of year rage almost each evening in the mountains, are very local, and while one stream may be a raging torrent, another only a mile away may be at normal level. At the time of our arrival the storms in the hills had been more than usually widespread and the Club Secretary's enquiries by telephone showed that at that time one stretch of river, and one only, held out any prospects. This was a stretch of rapid water flowing through the farm of New England and forming part of the head waters of the Ngwangwana River. It lay about twenty-five miles from Himeville and for it on the morning after our arrival we set out by car. In the event it was to prove that this part of the fishing was indeed for a time the only stretch of the Club water which was and remained fishable and altogether we paid it four visits while the river fell rapidly from being very high and coloured to being low and clear.

The surroundings of the New England water are very beautiful. At the bridge where we left the car each day we were hemmed in on either side by steep green hills rising to 7,000 or 8,000 feet with rocky outcrops and low trees marking the course of the streams which fell in cascades between the wet rocks. Upstream the river emerged in the middle distance from lower wooded hills which rose to higher rocky tops and behind these again rose the sheer rocky faces, ridges and peaks of the Drakensberg looking like the Cuillins in Skye on a huge scale. The whole scene, meadows, woods and hills was clear cut and sparkling through the air washed by the night's storms, but across the rock faces of the final ridges rags of white cloud not yet sucked up by the strengthening sun, drifted and trailed. Above the bridge the river ran in white rapids, tiny falls and long pools. It might well have been one of the small sea-trout rivers of Western Inverness-shire or Ross-shire, a similarity made more striking by the fact that in many places the banks were fringed and overhung with a tall heather-like shrub looking in the distance exactly like rank heather. Below the bridge, the river changed its character. Here were still many rocky pools and runs, but there were smoother slower stretches too where the river turned and twisted among willows and other waterside trees and shrubs. If in the upper stretches one might imagine oneself in Wester Ross, here in places one might be in Hampshire. Only in the meadows back from the river banks did any comparison fail, for even Hampshire water-meadows in July could not rival the lushness and density of the growth nor could show dwarf iris and montbretia which grew scattered through the grass with arum lilies in the damp places.

The trout at New England were not large and all were rainbow. On our first two visits when the stream was still full we fished with a large wet fly—between large sea-trout and small salmon size—well sunk as we had been warned to do; for the water at this time of year is warm and the trout seek the deeper shaded pools where they tend to lie and feed far below the surface. This method may perhaps lack something in interest, but it is relatively effective, though on these first two visits we only got four keepable fish, between ½ and ¾lb, putting back a number of smaller ones and having many touches. We returned to New England on two more occasions, by which time the water had fallen very greatly. These visits only added two more keepable trout, but we found that now when the water was shallow and clear the trout would take a dry fly right up in the rapid water at the necks of the pools. These fish in the shallow streams were small and all had to be returned, but it was a pleasure to see them rising to a floating fly instead of only feeling the tug of an underwater fish. Looking back on it we were grateful to the New England water for providing us with fishing when we could have got it nowhere else and showing us one of the most lovely of the many beautiful glens which we saw on our travels.

As the days passed, another of the streams partially controlled by the Fishing Club came gradually into fishable condition. This was the River Polela which passes under the main road half a mile from Himeville. We did not fish the upper waters of the Polela but concentrated our efforts on the several miles of water below the bridge. Here the river, except in a few places where it crosses outcrops of rock, has almost entirely the character of an English dry fly stream. The water even in dry weather is slightly cloudy in colour and the golden gravel of the chalk stream is missing, but for the rest it glides with a

swift but smooth flow between willow-fringed banks. These banks are not tended and there are very many places where bushes overhanging the water or flotsam caught on their branches trailing on the surface make many a likely corner virtually unfishable. Here, too, the flat land bordering the stream is covered with tall reeds and grasses and thick herbage of all kinds the passage of which under a blazing sun and a shade temperature in the eighties or nineties makes a day's fishing quite arduous.

In these lower and deeper stretches of the river the method of fishing with a rather large wet fly well sunk is, at least in the South African summer months, almost always used. We were told that sometimes in April and May or again in September, which are the best fishing months, trout may be seen rising freely to natural flies on the surface and that then a dry fly may be profitably used; but we saw practically no fish feeding on the surface and few natural flies save dragon-flies. The first day we fished the Polela the river was still full and the water very clouded. Few fish were rising and we came near success on only one pool. This was a long deep pool with a swift flow in at the neck and a slow section in the middle becoming more rapid towards the tail. Near the tail of the pool where a tiny stream came in a trout touched my deep-sunk fly but did not take it. Going a little way back I fished over the same water and again he came at me deep down. This time he was hooked and for a pleasant half minute I was playing a very strong trout which seemed from the glimpse I had of him to be about 1½lb; but the fish was not well hooked and soon broke free. My friend who was fishing below later tried the pool and in the same place hooked what seemed almost certainly the same trout, only to have the same experience. After fishing these streams for some days it seemed to me that the main difficulty lay in the firm hooking of the fish. When they took, they did so gently and almost tentatively. One hardly knew they were there and consequently did not strike firmly as one would do to a more active and visible rise. The right technique on feeling a fish seemed to be to wait for a second or two and then strike hard.

Our main success on the Polela came some days later when the level of the river had fallen considerably and the water had cleared. Fish were moving freely though still not feeding on the surface. When the light was right we could see them following the fly and though we touched and lost many we ended the day with six, of which the largest was 1½lb. If these fish took slowly and tentatively they were active enough when hooked. We had many exciting and anxious moments among the tall reeds and the trailing willows and the trout we got were all in beautiful condition.

One more river we fished was the Loteni River about fifteen miles from Himeville. One of the many kind friends we met at Himeville owned a sheep farm far up the valley of the Loteni and to this we went on two occasions. Neither of these expeditions was successful from the fishing point of view, for the river which is a rapid one was too full and there were at that time practically no pools where the fly had a chance. I chiefly remember these visits from the extreme beauty of the river and valley which reminded me so much of the upper stretches of Glen Etive in Argyllshire, and by the fact that on the second occasion we were driven out by the greatest heat I have ever felt.

Looking over the rolling grassland from the rising ground behind Himeville one saw the gleam of many lochs, and in fact nearly every farm had one on its ground. The Government encourages the building of these artificial lochs, or dams as they call them, as potential sources of irrigation and watering of stock, and the cost of their building is, I understand, treated for tax purposes as a farm outlay. Many of these are stocked with rainbow trout and in our first days at Himeville, when only the New England water was fishable, we paid two visits to a large dam about thirty miles from Himeville, lying on exposed ground at a height of about 7,000 feet. On the first day our fishing started rather disastrously. In Durban I had bought a number of nylon casts which I was assured were appropriate for rivers or dams. These were tapered to points of 5lb breaking strain. The first trout I hooked went straight away from the boat tearing out line, found a tough weed round which it twisted my line and then broke the cast with no bother. So did the next two. All were big fish and I was more than a little vexed. Thereafter I resorted to salmon casts which were luckily in my cast case and had no further breakages, though even the thicker gut was well tested. Some of these fish we caught by casting and pulling in the line slowly and deep-sunk. A number, I must admit, were caught by trolling, but the difference between trolling and pulling in a sunk line seems to me a slight one raising not much of a moral issue. We ended the day with over a dozen trout averaging nearly 1½lb. Four days later we again went there—a day of blazing sun and strong wind in which the flat-bottomed boat was almost uncontrollable. My wife was with us and she

I

was responsible for most of the catch which included a lovely fish of 2¾lb. Another dam on which we fished lay about six miles from Himeville. On our first visit we got to this loch at 6 am. Natal people are early risers and we had been told that the trout in McDougall's Dam were the same. We did not find it so, and though the water looked perfect with a lovely ripple we saw nothing except some most interesting birds. On our second visit we were driven off by an absolute cataract of rain and got back as wet as if we had been swimming, but in that warm climate none the worse. Our third visit was more successful, for my wife got a trout of just under 4lb after a long struggle, and I lost another big fish.

The Himeville/Underberg area, so near the hills but surrounded by rolling grassland, dotted with woods and lochs and watered by deep-flowing streams, was an ideal area for birds. Nearly all these were, at first, entirely strange to us, but as the days passed we were able with the aid of binoculars and an African bird-book to identify quite a number. Of the large birds of prey we saw many circling far up among the hills. Some of these were vultures of various types, with buzzards and kites and possibly eagles. Just before our first visit to the high-lying dam to which I have referred a cow had been killed by lightning and lay on the open hillside about a quarter mile from the water's edge. On that first day a number of vultures were circling above, some, with jackal buzzards waiting their turn, were hard at work on or in the carcass, and by the time of our second visit two days later little was left but the skin hanging on the ribs. In addition to the ordinary kite, which is a relatively large brown bird with long forked tail, we saw sitting on fences or telephone wires numbers of the much smaller black shouldered kite. Why it is so named is not clear, for this lovely bird, smaller than a sparrow hawk, is mainly a pale slate blue with pure white breast. There were kestrels, too, and other smaller hawks, and the first time we went to New England I put up from the riverside a pair of Cape pheasants, only a little bigger than our partridge. They had hardly got into the air when a hawk swooped on one of them. The pheasants dropped like stones into the grass—and just made it. In the meadows, particularly near the rivers, were very many large birds, mainly of the wader or long-legged type. Herons, storks and geese were a common sight, with cranes of various types. At Mc Dougall's Dam the day my wife caught the big trout we were lucky enough to see several of the very large black and white wattled crane, the cock birds apparently engaged in a mating display; but one of the most lovely of the large birds we saw was the crowned crane. We were driving the car very slowly down to the Polela River through meadow land where the grass and reeds came almost up to the roof of the car and only the faintest track showed the existence of the slightly raised road-way which we were following with more faith than confidence. On a slight slope 100 yards off we saw these huge birds which we were able to study closely through binoculars. They seemed to stand nearly three feet high at the shoulder with another eighteen inches of neck and head. The back and tail were slate coloured with white and deep yellow on the lower part of the body. On the neck immediately below the beak was a patch of vivid red, while the head was black with a lovely golden crest erect and extending from front to back. The patches of bramble and low scrub beside the river were alive with the tiny bishop bird whose chest looks as if covered with jet black velvet, while head and back are brilliant yellow or in some cases flaming red. The smaller birds as a whole were surprisingly tame and often we could study them from only a few yards. One day when fishing at New England from the top of a steep sandy bank I noticed a sand-martin anxiously flying back and forward just below me with a grass in her mouth. I moved on a step, when she immediately disappeared into a nesting hole almost at my very feet. In the meadows were quail and guinea-fowl, by the riverside sand-pipers and an occasional kingfisher, while on the fences and telegraph wires sat shrikes and quantities of swallows and martins—the two latter clearly talking over plans for early migration.

Often as we walked or motored through the meadow land we would see what in the distance seemed to be a black rag fluttering on a fence or apparently suspended just over the tall grass. This was the black widow-bird, of which we saw two varieties, one with vivid orange patches on neck and shoulders, the other black and white. In both

varieties the cock bird in the mating season grows a long black tail—
18 inches long in the orange patched variety. This tail hangs suspended
below the bird as it hovers, apparently with difficulty, over the grass
where it is presumed that the hen—in drab brown plumage—crouches
lost in admiration. We were never tired of watching what is really
a fantastic display. The cock widow-bird in full plumage and long
tail must measure 2 feet overall and yet it is so light that it can land with
ease on many of the tall meadow weeds and grasses. We were seldom
able to identify the songs and calls of the birds which we heard in the
woods and the riverside bushes. On the whole we formed the impression that the South African birds as songsters are inferior to our own,
but one which we constantly heard but never identified had a most
lovely liquid wood-wind note. This, with the never ending churr of
the small dove and the sound of cricket, grasshopper and cicada recall
most vividly the African twilight.

Altogether we were almost a month in the Himeville area and when
the time came to return to Durban we did so with real regret.
We had fallen in love with the grassy plateau, the deep streams and
the view of the mountains, always changing as the clouds drifted and
cleared and massed again for the evening storms. As for the fishing,
we knew that we had come at the wrong season for much success,
but we felt that we had learned a lot and were well on the way to
some degree of proficiency.

On our return to Durban we handed back the car which we had
hired and took the night train to Johannesburg. Here we spent a short
weekend and then got a magnificent air-conditioned train which took
us in twenty-five hours to Capetown. After two days in Capetown
we set out for Lanzerac which is on the outskirts of the pleasant university town of Stellenbosch, 30 miles north-west of Capetown.
Rawdon's Hotel, Lanzerac, is a picturesque estate mansion house built
in the Dutch style filled with much old furniture and dating back to
1820. It stands on the edge of vineyard country which here stretches
for many miles, for Stellenbosch and the neighbouring town of Paarl
are almost at the centre of the South African wine making industry.
The grape harvest was in full swing. Wherever we went we passed

through vineyards with black and green grapes hanging in tight clusters. Lorries loaded with mounds of picked grapes bound for the crushing plants constantly passed us on the roads.

South of Stellenbosch and looking north over the wide stretch of vineyard country are the Drakenstein Mountains, rising to 5,000 feet of rock face, peak and ridge. Rawdon's Hotel lies at the foot of a narrow glen—Jonkershoek Valley—running several miles back into these hills. In this part of Cape Province many of these glens are reserved as Forestry Areas. Jonkershoek Glen is one such area, and as many of the streams we hoped to fish run through ground controlled by the Department of Forestry, we had on our way from Capetown got a permit to enter and fish in forest land. Jonkershoek, lying so near Stellenbosch University, has in addition to a Forestry Research Station a Fish Hatchery and a Nature Reserve, so it is a centre of varied activity and considerable interest. We found the Head Forester most interesting and helpful and spent many pleasant hours far up the forest road which circles the glen. The trees grown here are almost all pines of various kinds, mostly native to the west coast of America, and looking up the glen with planted areas at various stages of growth running up the hillside we were constantly reminded of the Forestry Commission areas on the west coast of Scotland. The trees grow much quicker than with us, and at Jonkershoek we were shown stands 50 feet tall almost ready for their final thinning, and yet we were told that they were only about fifteen years old. Franschoek was another long valley near Stellenbosch controlled by the Forestry Department which we explored in search of fishing. Forest roads led in all directions and for most of one hot afternoon we followed one after another far up towards the head of the glen and directly under the high rock faces, hardly knowing where we were going, but content to enjoy the absolute quiet and shade of the forest.

The fishing round Stellenbosch—and indeed throughout Cape Province—is in complete contrast to that in the Natal Highlands. In Natal our chief enemy had been floods and discoloured water. It is true that when we first went to Stellenbosch there was a period of heavy rain when the river was in flood and the grape farmers in despair, but this was exceptional and short-lived and for the most part the rivers were low and brilliantly clear. With only two weeks in the Cape and only part of that time available for fishing it would be absurd to claim that we had acquired any extensive knowledge of trout fishing in the Cape. We did, however, get to know quite a bit about two typical rivers and through the very helpful Cape Piscatorial Society in Capetown accumulated a lot of general information. Down the glen which lay behind Rawdon's Hotel at Lanzerac ran the little River Eerste. It is a clear mountain stream about the size of the river which reaches the sea at Kentallen just south of Ballachulish, its bed a mass of great boulders and smooth rounded granite stones. Though it runs through a forest area, the forest trees do not extend to the river. While this is so, however, the stream is very nearly overgrown with willows and other bushes growing among the stones and boulders, and when we first explored it we reached the conclusion that at least in its upper stretches it was quite unfishable. This view was only slightly modified on a second inspection, but by dint of local enquiries and some rather perilous exploration we did find a few places where it was possible to throw either a dry or a wet fly. We eventually found, too, a short stretch of the river where it flowed through scattered woods rather nearer Lanzerac where by wading up the bed of the stream it was possible to cast a fly. So far as the Eerste is concerned this is not a success story, and it will suffice to say that by considerable effort we caught about a dozen rainbow trout, partly with dry fly and partly with wet. These were mostly small, and though two or three of these were above the size limit of 9 inches we returned them all. We explored, too, a stretch of the river near where it reaches the sea. Here the river is broader, slower and rather muddy. On our only visit to this stretch when the flow, reduced by abstraction of water for irrigation, was relatively small we decided that fishing would be both dull and unprofitable—a view shared by a homesick woman from Sutherland, the wife of a nearby fruit farmer. We did not attempt to fish here, though I understand that the rainbow trout at certain seasons migrate to the salt water and that in suitable conditions and high water large trout may be caught with a large sunk fly.

By far the most interesting fishing expeditions we made when at Lanzerac were to a much larger river 25 miles away. Between Stellenbosch and the large fruit growing area round Worcester the Great National Road climbs to a height of 2,900 feet to cross a pass in a high ridge of the Drakenstein Mountains. After reaching the summit, where one gets a wonderful view back to Table Mountain and the sea, the road tunnels through the hillside and emerges into a narrow rocky glen. The hills rise almost sheer on either side and we felt bound to admit that neither Glencoe nor Torridon nor Glenshiel could equal the wildness of the scene. On our first visit to Du Toit's Kloof—for such is its name—mist and heavy rain enveloped the top of the pass and in the glen the cloud level was low. The rock faces on each side disappeared into the mist from which many waterfalls fell hundreds of feet sheer to the Kloof and the river below. At one point I counted ten such falls. Many were quite large streams, but so strong was the wind at the time that the falling water was blown up or across, finally reaching the foot of the high cliffs only as clouds of spray and mist. The river that day was in full spate and we did no fishing. Three days later we returned with our rods. A short way from the end of the tunnel in the Kloof, a large tributary, the Elandspad, joins the Du Toit River. The Elandspad comes down from the hills in a rocky narrow glen with lovely deep pools near its junction with the main river. On the day we fished it the stream was full after the rain, but not too high for fly fishing, slightly coloured and apparently in perfect condition. The rocky bed, steep banks and undergrowth made fishing very arduous, but all through the forenoon we fished up through these lower pools with wet fly—and no success. Towards midday we came to a place where the river took a turn under a high rock face on the near side while opposite was a very steep hillside covered with huge tumbled boulders and overgrown with dense bush. The pool itself was deep and unwadeable and clearly we could go no farther. Returning to the main road through extreme heat, we made for a small inn a little way down the glen for the drinks we so badly needed. On learning of our failure the innkeeper suggested that we should have been using a dry fly and we arranged to come again a few days later to fish the main river.

Our next visit to the Du Toit River was some three days later by which time both the Elandspad and the main river had fallen very greatly. This time we motored down to the small hotel and fished the part of the river immediately adjoining it. The river here was very much bigger than the Eerste—a swift stream of brilliantly clear water in a broad bed filled with the massive boulders and large smooth rounded stones typical of these hill streams. The river bank itself was not so wooded and overgrown as the Eerste, but the difficulty was to get to it. For at nearly every point one had to force one's way through shoulder-high grass and bush growing among boulders. Only here and there had some vestige of a track been made, and it was soon obvious that the only way to fish the river was to get into the bed of the stream and wade up. Even this was far from easy as it meant endless climbing over or around the great boulders between which were deep pools and pot-holes.

Our time in the Cape was now running short and we had only this one day to try out the Du Toit River as a dry fly stream. Yet in that time our apprenticeship made fairly rapid strides and though we killed only two trout—lovely fish of about ¾lb each—we rose five of which we hooked four. In that clear water the comparatively slow approach of these rainbow trout to the fly was often plainly visible and the habit of striking quickly, learned among Scottish trout on Scottish rivers, accounted for most of our losses. Here as on the Eerste and before at Himeville we used principally a Greenwell's Glory. I wonder if there is any part of the world where trout will not rise well to the Greenwell? I have now fished in many waters both in the United Kingdom, in Ireland and in Europe and have yet to find one.

We stopped fishing in the early afternoon. The heat in that narrow valley was very great and as we worked our way slowly up the river through all these hazards it became increasingly clear that for us, unused to this combination of fishing and rock climbing it was only a matter of time till we broke a rod or a limb or both. Still, our success, very modest though it was, at least showed us how these trout could be caught and made us feel that with a little more time and practice we could have acquired some proficiency. One other hazard, if it did not exactly deter us, was often at the back of our minds, and this was the risk of snakes. They told us that snakes are not as a rule found beside the rivers, at least in damp ground or among thick grass where they cannot move easily. For all that we did hear of trout fishermen being bitten or having narrow escapes, and it is certainly true that snakes like to lie on the warm rocks beside or over which we so constantly passed when fishing. It is only fair to say that we only saw three snakes during our time in South Africa. None of these was near a river and all seemed as scared as we felt.

The corner of the Elandspad where the deep pool and the steep rocks had barred our upstream progress is indeed the highest point to which the ordinary fisherman can go; but it is far from being the upward limit for those suitably equipped. In fact, many miles of excellent fishing water lie upstream well stocked with rainbow trout of 1 to 2½lb. Of this we only learned on our return to Capetown, though had we known of it earlier we could not have profited by the knowledge. For penetration to the middle and upper waters of the Elandspad is a major operation which only a very small number have achieved. The few parties who have done it with success have consisted of not less than three men equipped with supplies for several days, and particularly with rubber rafts or Li-lo mattresses for negotiating the many narrow gorges. These gorges are numerous, often 50 to 100 yards in length, of great depth and enclosed on either side by unclimbable rock walls. The food and other equipment is loaded on the raft which then is pushed or paddled up the gorge by one of the party swimming or lying on the raft. Between the gorges the rafts, rods and equipment have to be carried over the rocks and boulders which fill the bed of the stream. It is essentially a young man's sport, and even so there must be comparatively few who would be prepared to face the ardours and the undoubted risks. The proportion of fishing to swimming, rock climbing and other activities must be small, but the thrill of fishing in these virgin waters for strong wild trout must be very great.

CHAPTER 13

Two days on the Test

Two weeks had passed since the day in the third week of May when the trout in the Perthshire hill burn had risen so readily to the floating fly, and now I was on my way to fish the Test. Train journeys from Waterloo or Paddington never fail to recall for me happy days in the water-meadows, and as we passed through Fleet and Winchfield and on through the grass lands of east Hampshire, Patrick Chalmers' verses kept running in my mind:

> Pan doth pipe to us anew
> Reedy calls and catches
> So we'll go and throw a fly
> Dainty, delicate and dry
> Forty miles from Waterloo
> Where the may-fly hatches.

In fact, may-fly does not appear on the upper beats of the Test which

I was going to fish—but no matter. I was going to cast a fly. Whether it would be dainty or delicate remained to be seen. At least it would be dry.

The last week of May and the early days of June had been wet and stormy—no weather for dry fly fishing—and as we watched that night the television programme which commemorated the twentieth anniversary of the Normandy landings the wind moaned round the house below the Downs as it must have moaned on that June night of 1944 when the invasion plans with all that depended on them hung in the balance.

The morning of 6th June showed little improvement. The wind still blew hard from the south-west driving up the Test Valley banks of low cloud which promised rain later in the day. It was not a day to look for a large or early hatch of fly and when we reached the river at 11.30 there was still little sign of activity. As we stood on the bridge taking stock I looked downstream to the big ash tree near which on about the same day in the previous year a large trout lying in rapid water below a weed bed had scorned my best efforts as it fed on secure in the knowledge that my fly would inevitably drag. Below that again there lay, I knew, a stream which had witnessed another failure, this time owing to an over-quick strike at a rising fish with which I soon parted company. Would I be able to profit by the lessons of last year and improve on the results? I felt some doubt.

But today we were to fish the beat above the bridge, and to it we turned our attention. Down in the park through which this beat of the Test flows, the big trees now in full leaf broke the force of the wind so that only a moderate breeze blew up the river. The cooing of pigeons in the riverside trees and the distant sound of a cuckoo brought a sense of peace and high summer. Though there was no sun, some warmth had come as the morning passed and a few flies were appearing. There was nothing approaching a real hatch now, or indeed at any time during this day, but a number of fish were to be seen. Some were on or near the bottom and were clearly not, or not yet, taking any interest in food; but some were poised nearer the surface and at long intervals would rise. Some thirty yards above the bridge a good light-coloured fish had taken up its position in midstream near the top of a narrow strip of gravel beside a weed bed. He was clearly feeding if only spasmodically, and as we watched he would suddenly move to right or left to inspect or eat something not visible to us, occasionally making a rise. Of the trout in sight he seemed our best hope and to him we decided to lay siege. Between the bridge and our trout lay several other fish, which if disturbed would inevitably dash off upstream spreading alarm and despondency. So making a short detour through the buttercups and ragged-robin of the meadow, we carefully approached the edge of the river a few yards below the feeding trout, partially screened by the fringe of tall waterside plants which had been spared for this purpose from the scythe of the water keeper. The swift flow of the stream at this point made it inevitable that the fly would drag unless cast from almost directly below, so it was necessary to step down into the water—here only knee deep—and edge slowly out into midstream. The upstream breeze made casting easy and during the next half hour that trout had every chance. A fly passing directly over him was completely ignored, but those to right or left seemed for some reason to have more attraction. Every now and then he would turn to inspect what we offered him and very occasionally would follow the fly downstream apparently on the verge of taking it; but each time it failed to pass inspection and the trout would return to its original station. Like a test match captain, we varied our attack with the smallest of hackle flies and nymphs. At least it was to some extent a drawn battle for the trout continued to feed and we did not have the humiliation of putting him down; but neither did we make him rise. It is always a difficult question how long to persevere at a feeding fish in the hope that you may wear him down, but by now a few fish were to be seen rising farther up the river and we decided to write him off as being what Plunkett-Greene fishing at Hurstbourne Priors only a few miles off once described as a 'time waster', and moved slowly on.

A short way above the time waster another trout was lying near the edge of a weed bed. He was rather smaller than his colleague below but looked like a keepable fish and as he was clearly on the look-out for flies we decided to fish for him. This trout was a good deal farther over towards the far bank and to reach a point directly below would have meant serious disturbance of the water, which, with the trout so unsettled as they were, we could not risk. But here the flow of the stream was slightly slower and there was proportionately less risk of drag. A few cautious steps into the edge of the stream put me in position and soon this second trout was under fire. At first he took no notice and it seemed that he too would defeat us; but like our first opponent this trout was interested in flies passing beside rather than over him. A lucky cast a foot or so to one side stirred his fancy and turning downstream he followed and finally rose to the tiny hackled fly. The length of line and perhaps some vestige of my resolution to strike slowly had their effect and this trout was firmly hooked. If the trout of the chalk stream are more difficult to approach and harder to rise than those of northern streams—and almost certainly they are—once hooked, the battle is in many cases more than half won. The life of a chalk stream trout centres largely on the weed beds beside which he feeds and to which in time of trouble he retires. When hooked, his first and almost his only thought is to bury himself in weed, but in open water he lacks the cunning or the strength of a trout living in colder waters. This trout was no exception. He made from one weed bed to another, but the luck and the fine cast held, and after a few anxious moments he was in open water and soon in the net. A fine thick-set trout of $1\frac{1}{4}$lb—of good average weight for these upper beats.

Success so early in the day seemed to promise a good basket and soon a second trout which was rising a short way above was on the bank. Though rather smaller than our first trout he was well over 1lb, so now we had a brace; and when almost immediately after we got a third, it seemed almost too good to be true; but this third fish looked to be under our 12 inch limit, so rather regretfully we let him go.

Tall trees growing to the water's edge barred further progress up that side of the stream, so recrossing the bridge we made our way up the right bank of the river. Soon we came to a weir where the full concentrated flow of the Test passes under the hatches in a rush of

white water spreading out below into a broad stream of clear shallow
water rippling and hurrying over gravel beds of white and gold.
In this shallow water a trout would rise now and then, but flies were
not yet on the water in any number, and though we watched for a
long time we could find no steadily feeding trout for which to fish.
Above, the river, partially dammed by the weir, was smoother and
deeper, and with a long stretch in view beyond we sat to eat our lunch.

A little way above where we sat a large elm tree leaned over the
stream from the far bank and here in the half shadow a trout rose once
and then again. It lay beside a dark weed bed in rippling water where
it was difficult to see; but now and then as he moved to the side to inspect a fly or some insect in the water he came into clearer view and
we saw him to be a good trout and quite certainly a feeding one.
Between the near bank and the place where the trout lay the even
flow of the stream was broken by underwater weeds. The faster water
lay on the near side and a fly thrown across it would inevitably drag
almost as soon as it touched the surface. So here again we were faced
with the necessity of a cast from directly below.

My friend and host had insisted that on this, the first of my two precious days on the river, I should do the fishing; so once again I crept
downstream and waded slowly into the river well below the feeding
trout. Fortunately, no other fish were disturbed, or if they were they
fled downstream and soon I was in position. From here the difficulty
of seeing the feeding fish was very great, but my friend had remained
nearly opposite to it and was able to watch my fly and the reactions of
the trout. The subsequent campaign was not unlike our siege of the
first trout of the day but complicated by the fact that this fish lay perilously near the far bank where an inaccurate cast or an unlucky gust of
wind would land the fly on the tall grasses growing from the bank.
But a trout rising near the bank at least gives you the advantage that
even when you cannot see him continuously you can pinpoint his
position fairly accurately, and soon a fair number of my casts were
putting the fly over or very near where he lay. As I fished, my friend
kept up a running commentary; now he would report that the trout
had turned to look at my fly, again that he was even following it

but more often that no notice was being taken. But the trout was still clearly feeding and as he was a good one and feeding trout that day were scarce we persevered. We changed the fly, substituting a small snipe and purple for the blue upright. The results were no better and I had almost given it up as hopeless when the trout moved a little way to one side giving a clearer view of him against the weed bed. I cast again and the fly came over him. Suddenly he disappeared from my sight and I thought he had at last taken fright, but in fact he had followed the fly downstream and rose to it unexpectedly some feet below his usual feeding place. This time he meant to have it and was firmly hooked. He ran downstream past me and fought hard and well, but we got him in the end. He weighed 1½lb, a lovely fish and very well worth all the time and trouble he had cost us.

Three good trout in the bag by early afternoon is, on a chalk stream, a matter for some satisfaction, and we faced the rest of the day with not unnatural but, as it proved, misplaced confidence. A short way above us the river took a slight bend and from the corner we could see up a long meadow to a second hatch hole a quarter of a mile upstream. Down by the waterside the wind had fallen, but above our heads low clouds still moved steadily in from the south-west. The hatch of fly is always unpredictable and will occur in almost any conditions; but perhaps a heavy atmosphere with no sun and little lightness in the air is the least favourable for fly to appear. Certainly at no time on that day did flies hatch in any number. Yet as we looked up that long stretch of the water we could see what seemed to be the rise of trout at fairly regular intervals and our hopes rose high; but not for long. For the trout of the upper Test had on that June day judged the position more accurately than we had, and in the absence of flies had taken to more profitable if less exciting pursuits. What we saw were indeed feeding trout, but trout feeding not on surface food but on shrimps and other delicacies in the gravel beds of the shallows. So engrossed were they that we were able to approach quite close to some of them as they stood almost literally on their heads, the edges of their broad tails emerging from the water. The trout has many habits which at times drive the fisherman almost to distraction, but few can be more frustrating than this habit of feeding in the gravel. The sight of a trout's tail cutting the surface of the water seems to make him appear larger than perhaps he really is, and the realisation that he is almost certainly immune from legitimate capture makes the tribulattions of Tantalus seem as nothing. I say 'legitimate capture' advisedly, for watching the antics of these large trout I was reminded of a far-off autumn day on the Itchen a few miles above Winchester. It was late October and the fishing season was long past; but we had gone up the river on a leave-out day from school to watch the trout. The water keeper had been wiring pike and he sent us off equipped with long bamboo poles with nooses of snare wire at the ends to try our luck. The pike were hard to find and very wary, but after a time we came on a stretch of shallow water where trout were gravel feeding with their tails above the surface. The devil entered into us and soon a trout of about a pound and a half suffered the indignity of leaving the Itchen tail first. In fairness to ourselves I should add that it was hurriedly returned to the water.

As the afternoon passed we made our way slowly up that long meadow of the upper Test looking in vain for rising fish and seeing only gravel feeders steadily at work. At some of these we could not resist throwing a fly in the faint hope that they might be distracted from their occupation. We might as well have been throwing stones at them. Soon a light drizzle started to fall turning gradually to steady rain. The day was over and we turned downstream. Above the bridge the time waster was still visible near his weed bed but now we had no hope of him and we left him to his own devices.

During the night the wind fell, the rain cleared and we woke to a day of better promise; but the clouds were still low and there seemed little prospect of sun. Today we were to fish a beat above the one we had fished the previous day, and this time my hostess and her two small daughters were to come with us for a short time in the hope of seeing a trout caught. An audience however charming and uncritical, especially on a chalk stream where nerves are tense, is apt to be upsetting and I felt far from confident that I could provide them with anything worth watching, even if a feeding trout could be found.

But this morning the Gods were with me. We came to the river at the tail of a long pool. At its head the river ran swift and narrow under overhanging willows broadening out into smoother and deeper water below. In the swift water under the willows we could see more than one good trout near the surface, occasionally making a rise, but the willows and the swift stream combined to make them almost unassailable, only to be attempted if nothing easier were to be found. In the smoother water below the neck of the pool a second trout lay beside a weed bed about thirty yards above us. Though not as yet rising, he was poised near the surface and we were about to move up to within casting distance when we noticed a third and much larger trout closer to us as we crouched behind the fringe of tall riverside grasses. This trout lay in deep smooth water and though not very near the surface he had a certain air of watchfulness and seemed worth a cast before we attacked his colleague above. The slight wind blew upstream, the cast was not a long one, and the only obstacles were the racing heart and the trembling hand of an over-eager fisherman watched by four spectators praying for his success. The first cast fell short but the second was an answer to prayer and the fly came right over him. He turned upwards, came slowly and deliberately to the surface and took the fly with a leisurely businesslike rise. They say on this part of the Test that between the rise of a trout and the strike one should say 'God Save the Queen'. I doubt whether I managed much more than 'God'—which perhaps expressed not inadequately what in all the circumstances I felt; but it was enough. He was firmly hooked and fled downstream past us. That trout might have known that his capture was intended as a show-piece. He fought long and hard in full view of his audience except when for one horrid moment he bored into the weeds of the near bank under our very feet. From these he was at last forced out again into clear water and soon a lovely trout of $1\frac{3}{4}$lb was in the net. Here our audience left us. I was sorry to see them go, but perhaps felt some relief that they should go while an undeserved and yet untarnished reputation for skill and accuracy was still at the zenith.

The feeding trout under the willows proved, as we had feared,

K

uncatchable, but from the smooth water of the pool above my friend got a good fish with a speed and apparent lack of effort which made the operation appear deceptively easy. In the meadow beyond there were few signs of activity save for gravel feeders steadily at work. Here we sat to eat our lunch and smoke in the hope of fly appearing. For long we waited watching the water but no fly came and we turned down the stream.

A little way below the point where we had started that morning was a short stretch of water less often fished. Here were larger and more frequent weed beds, while trees and willows overhung part of the water. Altogether this was more difficult water to fish but we had some hope that if any trout were rising here they might prove less selective and more interested in what we had to offer them. At first we could find only gravel feeders of which we could make nothing, but soon we came to more rapid water where a good trout was rising in a swift stream beside a weed bed. While my friend attacked it from below I kept watch well back from the bank but nearly opposite the trout. For long he ignored the flies passing over him, but a lucky change of pattern took his fancy and as the fly passed he chased and ate it. This was a good trout and almost a twin in shape and weight of my morning capture. Shortly after this we got another rather smaller, and then the day seemed over. A few fish were still rising at long intervals and with all but one we carried on intermittent but unproductive contests. With all but one. He lay at the edge of a weed bed near the far bank. A long cast, but a big trout. Two casts fell short but the third just reached him. The fly fell a few inches above him and almost as it fell he took it. Without a pause he shot upstream and buried himself in the depth of a weed bed 10 yards above. There was a moment of tension on the long line which I could not ease and then the fly came back. As I sadly reeled in I reflected on my hasty judgement of the fighting qualities of Test trout. One at least had proved me wrong.

CHAPTER 14

Autumn in the Ochils

This autumn of 1964, in our part of the country at least, will, I believe, be long remembered. September, so often the best month of our whole year, was cold, wet and very windy, and the harvest, good in quality and plentiful, was won in bits and pieces as the weather allowed. But with October the Indian Summer which the south had been enjoying came north. The wind fell, the sun shone, while light frosts at night brought colour to leaves which hung motionless in the still air.

The first to turn were the larches. The green of the needles lightened and yellowed and soon the sun shone on the pure gold of the European and hybrid varieties and the deeper russet of the Japanese. Close on the heels of the larches followed the birches, the beeches, the maples and the geans in every shade of yellow and gold and red. Nearer at hand the clumps of azaleas beside the house showed many colours, some bushes wine-coloured or blood-red, others a lovely mixture of reds and greens. Even the young shoots of the sycamore, which with us seldom greet the approach of autumn with more than black

139

spots on shrivelling leaves, turned to pale yellow. In the still days the leaves hung on the trees beyond their usual time and all through the woodlands and along the hedgerows the sun shone on a world of vivid colour.

Along the hedges at the edge of the woods the bramble patches had been white with blossom in the summer, but the bleak days of September had done little to ripen the crops and there seemed small prospect of filling the bottling jars or the jam and jelly pots; but the dry sunny days of October following the rain swelled and ripened the berries and turned the prospect of a poor gathering into the certainty of a bumper crop. At the foot of the hill below our house the bramble patch which borders a little stream grew black with fruit, and standing in the deep ditch we filled our baskets from the sprays of berries which hung over the stream, some bent by the weight of fruit to the very surface of the shallow water. Standing in the ditch, the water hardly covering the feet of our rubber boots, it was hard to credit that in this very place last autumn the foresters cleaning the edges of the ditch after a few days of heavy rain had caught, measured and returned to the stream a fish 3 feet 2 inches in length—a large spawning salmon which had somehow struggled up to this point from the river 3 miles away.

On the shoulder of the hill which overlooks the small loch a short way above our house an area of about four acres has been fairly recently planted with larch and Scots pine. Of the young trees, the larches now five years old have prospered and grown quickly. On the drier ground above them, however, the Scots pine have had a hard struggle. On the hillside were many patches of whin which had to be partially cleared before the trees were planted. The whin was the home of countless field mice which found the soft stems and buds of the young Scots pines a welcome source of food during the hard spring weather which followed their planting, while a blizzard of snow buried and broke many of the young trees and made deep drifts against the wire netting over which the blue and brown hares entered with ease to nibble the buds and shoots of the trees. Now, despite their early troubles, the young trees are mostly well established and growing fast, but among the pines especially, the evidence of their early misfortunes is only too apparent. In tree after tree the loss of the bud which would have grown into the leader has meant that the side branches are now competing for leadership; a competition, which if allowed to continue, will retard and in many cases permanently damage the growth of the tree.

So I have spent many hours of this lovely autumn weather clad in old clothes and carrying powerful clippers, examining the trees which have lost their leaders and doing what I can by rough and ready surgery to encourage the formation of a new leader. Sometimes it has been easy to decide on the steps required; but often the claims of several aspirants to leadership are closely balanced. Then one must judge as best one can which of the competitors has the best chance of development, remembering that where possible a branch turning in towards the hill should be preferred to one tending down-hill since the latter will make the tree in days to come more vulnerable to wind. Sometimes I have found it impossible to make a choice and have left the competing branches to fight it out in the hope that by another year the issue may have become more clear. It is interesting work and satisfying, for while it is sad to see so many trees struggling against troubles so early in life, there is the certainty that even if sometimes one makes the wrong decision very many of these young trees will have been greatly helped.

From the high shoulder above the loch where these young trees are growing one looks down on almost the whole length and breadth of Strathearn, 700 feet below. Beyond the valley is the line of the Grampians. Crieff and the Sma' Glen are nearly opposite and from behind the nearer ridges to the west of Crieff the top of Ben Lawers peeps over. Westward again are Ben Voirlich and Stuc-a-chroin and if I move only a few yards up the hillside the view will open to Ben Ledi and Ben Lomond. In many a year these high tops have already got their first covering of snow, but this year in the second week of November hardly a patch of snow is to be seen even on the highest ground—and many of the hills to which I look are 3,000 feet and more.

Today was a day of complete and breathless calm. The smoke of Auchterarder, of Crieff, and of the farms and cottages dotted over Strathearn rose straight in the air or hung in thin blue clouds and pools far above the houses. On the hills round the Sma' Glen and at the head of Glenlednock, gamekeepers and shepherds were making the most of the dry weather to burn the heather, and here and there rose pillars of blue smoke against the brown of the heather slopes.

At my feet the water of the small loch reflected as in a sheet of black glass the greens and golds of the surrounding trees. Out in the centre two coots made, with occasional late-rising trout, the only ripples on the surface. The coots have, at least in a domestic sense, had a successful season. Out of their eight eggs they reared to maturity five young birds and until the end of September the seven birds had all the appearance of being a happy united family. Then one day we visited the loch to find that only the two parent birds remained. There had, we felt sure, been no tragedy. The young birds were by that time fully grown and to all appearances able to fend for themselves. No foxes had been seen about the loch and no feathers or other remains were to be seen. No, it seemed to us certain that this had been a dispersal of the family according to Nature's plan and that the time had come when the young birds were due to be turned out into the world to seek their fortunes. But this raised interesting speculation as to how it had taken place. Had the decision been taken by the cock or the hen, or in some nocturnal discussion between the two? Had the hen, perhaps, pleaded for some delay till George or Mary (always backward children) had grown a little stronger? We shall never know, but away the young birds had gone, whether in ones and twos or in one homesick and bewildered group, and whether on wing or on foot—for coots are neither strong nor far fliers.

The young planting where I have been working covers the upper part only of the steep shoulder overlooking the loch. The lower part of the slope has hitherto been left unplanted so that the cattle grazing on the grasslands below could have access to it. But the cattle have seldom penetrated to it, preferring the richer grass of the lower fields, and the whin patches have been spreading. So this autumn we decided to plant this part also in the coming spring and now the foresters have been busy fencing in this lower part of the hill, fencing in also as it transpired a brown hare which had its home among the whins. The lower fence of the earlier planted ground, now no longer needed, has been removed and so within the new wire fence lie 4 acres of planted ground, 4 acres of open hillside awaiting planting, and one hare. It is a situation much to the liking of Judy our Aberdeen Terrier (an inveterate hare-chaser) who always comes with me—and indeed to the liking of all concerned. Judy has 4 acres of open grassland and whin clumps in which to hunt her hare. The hare has few worries for if at all hard pressed it can retire into the planted area where Judy's short legs can hardly carry her through the long grass and heather growing between the young trees. Meantime I have my work among the trees, Strathearn in all the beauty of these autumn days stretched far below me, and the certain knowledge that when I go home to lunch or in the falling light of the shortening days Judy will be not far off, well exercised and ready for her dinner, her basket or her corner of the sofa near the fire.

Today, to my regret, I almost finished my work among the young trees. I am loath to leave a spot so completely satisfying to man and beast—and perhaps I shall pay another visit to go through the planting once more and to let Judy and the hare have another run. Today as I worked, the grouse on the nearby hillside were very vocal, and now and then a cock would take a short flight to land in the heather only a few yards beyond the upper edge of the planting. Geese on passage between the Tay estuary, Loch Leven and the flat ground at the head of Strathallan passed and repassed far above me talking among themselves. Their constant movement and the shortening days remind me that winter is just round the corner; that the winds which must soon come will strip the leaves and the needles from so many of the trees and that this golden autumn will be at an end. The geese will move finally to their winter quarters down on the coast, while the surface of the loch will for a time be roughened and whitened by gales from the north-west till the frosts and the snow come to bring a new quietness and a different beauty to the Ochils.

CHAPTER 15

Dry fly above the Vale of Alford

Some twenty-five miles from its source on the borders of Banffshire and Aberdeenshire, the Aberdeenshire Don finally leaves the hills and enters the rich belt of farming land known as the Vale of Alford. In the last few miles before it leaves the higher ground, the river follows a devious course, with many twists and bends, as if loath to leave finally the high rounded hills which have, at least to this point, given it much of its character. Hitherto, the main road through Strathdon has followed the river for many miles from near its source, but shortly before the Don emerges from the hills, the road diverges for a time from it. So it comes that below this point there are several miles of the stream far from any buildings larger than a farm and a few cottages, approached and at long intervals crossed only by the quietest of farm roads.

It would be easy, and perhaps tempting, to single out one stretch of a river as what, in another context, might be called its 'heartland': but such a selection must clearly depend largely on the tastes and experience of the individual, and only subject to this can it have any general validity. Nonetheless, the few miles of river of which I write, twisting and turning between the heather, broom and whin-covered hills which it is so soon to leave, and above all far removed from even the modified movement and noise of the Donside road, have, I believe, more than a small claim to be regarded as in many ways the essence of Donside. For myself, at least, the beauties and characteristics go far to explain how the twists and turns of this part of the river have, in the course of many visits, bound so tightly my heart and my memory.

Other attractions of this stretch of the Don have certainly continued with its quietness and its natural beauty: its bird-life; its flowers, trees and shrubs, both by the waterside and on the hillsides; its trout, and above all its memories of friendship and kindness. Each has played its part. It would be hard indeed to assess the respective impact and influence of any one of them; and where in any event would be the object or the profit? Is it not better to accept with gratitude the gifts which Nature showers on us, rather than by over-analysis to risk spoiling any part of the pleasure which comes to us from the whole? So, I shall in retrospect touch only at random on some of the elements which go to make up the pleasure which this stretch of the Don has given me for many years past, making no attempt to rate any one of these higher than another.

A narrow side road, little more in parts than a cart track, turns off through a farm steading towards a bend in the nearby river. The road is largely unfenced, so that in the last five or six years during which my wife and I have gone this way so often we have in using the track passed successively through fields of turnips, hay, silage or pasture according as the rotation of crops has dictated. Our visits have been generally in the second half of May and often again about the middle of July, so that we have passed through fields not only of varied crops, but at varied stages of the growth of each; but at whatever time of year we have passed by, the bird life on either side of the road has always been fascinating in its variety and especially in its tameness. Perhaps the explanation of this lies largely in the nearness of the river, perhaps in the infrequency of such slow-moving agricultural traffic as passes, but sometimes we like to think that after the first few days the birds have come to look on us, if not as real friends, at least as harmless. On a recent visit in May, a nesting plover met us each morning at almost exactly the same spot, and latterly did no more than run a few steps from the passing car.

The track now turns along a steep bank overlooking the river. Here redshanks and sand-pipers are much in evidence, with mallard in the river directly below and on the riverside fence a lark sits undisturbed only a few feet from the car. In the centre of a neighbouring pasture field a mixed flock of gulls and oyster-catchers stand apparently in complete amity. Often as we pass, and more often as we fish, these lovely birds the oyster-catchers pass close overhead, the intense black and white of their plumage and the orange red of their long beaks combining with their peculiar ringing cry to proclaim their identity long before they pass overhead. But one great mystery attaches to them. Why does one so often see them in little groups of three, even in the mating season? There must clearly be some good reason, but none has ever been put forward, at least to my knowledge.

As we crossed the old bridge and turned upstream, our destination on a morning in late May of 1971 was a pool which we fish from the right bank and which lies close to the farm road. A sloping path leads from the road to a small piece of flat ground beside the river where a large flat boulder, the height of a low table, must have witnessed the fishing preparations, the frugal lunches, the joys and sorrows of generations of Donside anglers. The steep slope between road and river is covered with a thick growth of broom and wild rose, a joy to see when it is in bloom, but less admirable when a gust of wind or an ill-judged cast from the nearby river bank leaves line and cast in an almost inextricable tangle in a maze of twigs, thorns and branches which Nature might almost have designed for this express purpose. This tangle of wild rose and broom is a paradise for small birds of all kinds. We can identify with ease the yellow-hammer and some of the tits, while along the waterside itself grey and pied wag-tails, sand-pipers, plover and curlew are constantly passing; but almost hidden among the rose bushes and the broom are a range of small birds such as white-throats and several species of warbler whose presence is only betrayed by their song, which we are not knowledge-able enough to identify, and brief glimpses of movement among the bushes.

Above the road, directly at our backs as we fish, the hill climbs steeply for several hundred feet to a plantation of larch and Scots pine edged with a thick growth of whin and broom. The plantation and the bushes at its edge are full of pheasants, and for one sitting on the flat boulder beside the river, there seldom pass more than a few minutes when a cock pheasant is not to be heard, proclaiming its presence to the hens, challenging all comers, or merely putting into bird lan-guage the joy which all Nature must feel in a fresh, sunny morning of mid-May. Across the stream is a wide belt of ground covered with patches of willow and broom, whin and rushes, another paradise for feeding or nesting birds, and time and again a cock pheasant taking off from the plantation above passes overhead to land in this wild stretch of ground, after a gliding flight during the greater part of which it has hardly moved its wings. With all this wealth of bird life over and beside the river, I doubt whether there is another spot in Scotland where a greater number and variety of our indigenous birds could be seen or heard in so short a time and within such a short space.

A distinguished angler many years ago described the Don as a first-rate trout stream somewhat spoiled by the presence of a certain num-ber of salmon. Like so many generalisations, this one can only be ac-cepted subject to much qualification. It is most certainly true that compared with its neighbours the Dee and the Deveron, the Don, except possibly in a very few stretches of its lower course, does not even begin to compete as a salmon river, due, it seems probable to much pollution near its mouth. As a sea-trout river, the Deveron far surpasses in quality either of the other two, and it is only as a brown-trout stream that the Don emerges as a very real rival. In this capacity it far surpasses the Dee (though probably few people trouble to fish the Dee for trout) and at least equals the Deveron. This I believe is largely due to the presence up much of Donside of a belt of rich arable land with a marked limestone content. The latter is responsible both in the main stream and in many of the principal tributaries for a growth of weed, the home of quantities of snails and fresh-water shrimps on which the trout thrive. The lush growth on the banks of much of the middle and lower Don, too, is the breeding ground of flies which between the end of April and the middle of July may often be found hatching in quantities rivalling those to be seen in the water-meadows of Hampshire. Whatever the reason—and those suggested certainly play a large part—I believe it is true to say that in suitable conditions from early May to the middle of July there are days when the number, size and quality of trout to be caught on long stretches of the Don are hardly to be excelled anywhere in Scotland.

The pool below the farm road which we had come to fish on this May morning, is a case in point. The neck is shallow and strong, gradually deepening into the main body of the pool. As the water deepens and the size of the stones on the bed of the stream increases, this part of the pool becomes a regular salmon pool and many a fish has been taken from it over the years; but it holds many large trout as well, particularly in an eddy under the near bank rather more than half way down the pool. Here at times when flies are hatching, trout of 2 to 3lb may be seen cruising at the edge of the stream and in the backwater and eating flies at their leisure; but they are extremely difficult to catch, probably because the water in which they feed is very still, and they have all the time in the world to inspect a floating fly and to decide whether it is the genuine article. Lord Grey of Fallodon in his *Fly Fishing* describes how once in the long Mucomir Pool on the River Lochy he spent nearly a whole week fishing for salmon with a very heavy rod and large flies. He caught, it is true four salmon, none of them very fresh, and six grilse, besides a number of fresh-run sea-trout which, so far as sport was concerned were on his heavy rod utterly wasted. He confessed that were he faced again with the same situation he would be tempted to do again as he did, remembering the success of a friend who had once caught fourteen fresh-run salmon in this place on one day, and ignoring the knowledge that with a light rod and tackle he could have had magnificent sport with sea-trout of all sizes, besides almost certainly catching a few small salmon into the bargain. These, he writes, are some of the perplexities of sea-trout fishing in large rivers. Such certainly are the problems facing one who fishes a river such as the Aberdeenshire Don when salmon are in the river, and when large trout in considerable numbers are rising and are to be caught with a light rod and tackle either on a wet fly or a dry fly. Each angler must solve the problem for himself or herself in his or her own way, and it would be presumptuous to do more than point out what can sometimes be a cruel dilemma.

During the past season of 1971 conditions on the Don, and indeed on many other Scottish rivers, were quite exceptional. There had been almost no snow during the winter. The springs feeding the rivers were at a very low level, and little rain fell in the early springtime to fill them. So, when we arrived on Donside in mid-May the river was lower than almost anyone could remember. Even the kingcups and the forget-me-nots which at this time of year usually grow on the banks in profusion with their feet in the water were being hard put to it to survive with their roots almost uncovered. A few salmon had, it is true, struggled up earlier in the spring, but these unfortunately were nearly all diseased and all we saw in the way of salmon in a stretch of several miles of river were either dead or dying. So there was no temptation to fish for salmon rather than for trout, though even the latter, owing to the very low water, were hard to catch.

Good friends of ours who had been fishing in vain for salmon, before we arrived, and who knew how much pleasure I derive from fishing for trout with a dry fly suggested that I should explore a small but deep pool immediately above that already described beside the farm road; one which I had never thought worth trying. The pool was quite narrow. The main stream, strong-flowing even in these dry conditions, flowed down the far side; but on the near side was a much slower but very deep stretch of water which on closer inspection seemed promising, though no trout were rising. For many years I have fished the Don and other streams where dry fly can be used with a Greenwell's Glory tied as a hackle rather than a winged fly and on a large hook. The hackle fly, well dried and oiled when needed, floats well

even in very rapid water and the size of the fly makes it possible
to see it even at a considerable distance, a matter of no small importance
when sometimes all one sees is the sudden disappearance of the fly,
and an instant strike is vital. At the first full cast in the narrow pool,
the fly came floating down the near side of the stream at the very edge
of the deep water. Half way down the pool the fly disappeared with
only a slight indication of a break in the surface. A quick strike made
apparent that the hooked trout was a large one. In a moment it was
out in the swift current and running downstream with a speed and
power which I could do nothing to check. There are few things more
nerve-shattering for the trout fisherman than to be playing a large
fish far below him at the end of a long line ending in a point of only
about 3lb breaking strain. Fortunately, the bed of the stream immediately below was relatively clear of snags or large stones, so enabling
me to follow my fish quickly. Before long it had ceased to take out
line, and soon we were on fairly even terms, though the quick water
of the neck of the salmon pool below still favoured the trout. Luckily
my wife who was fishing for trout with wet fly a short distance below
me had seen my predicament. Hurrying up the bank with her
long-handled landing net she was able to get opposite the trout—
by now much exhausted—and the rest was easy. Returning to the
small deep pool I worked upstream and a few yards above where the
first trout had risen, a second rose to my fly, though in this case the
rise was much more visible and the size of the trout apparent. Its
tactics and ours on this occasion were almost identical to those adop-
ted by each of us previously and again after some anxious moments
the trout was in the net. The narrow pool was now thoroughly disturbed and no further trout rose in it; but the first one caught weighed
close on 2lb and the second only slightly less. Later, in the deep eddy
half way down the salmon pool where a few trout were still rising
quietly, we were able to induce one to make a mistake. He weighed
well over 2lb, so when we went home that evening it was with a
sense of at least some achievement.

A few days later I was walking slowly and somewhat disconsolately
downstream from the salmon pool beside the road. The sun shone,

the banks of broom and whin overlooking the river were golden masses, the wild roses were coming into bloom, while on the sides of the
road and on nearly every grassy bank exposed to the sun wild pansies,
blue and yellow and sometimes mixed, grew in greater profusion
than I had ever remembered to have seen them. All around were the
beauties of Nature; but no rain had fallen and the river was, if possible,
even lower and less promising than ever. The deep narrow pool where
I had got the two good trout a few days before had yielded nothing
and none of the monsters in the deep eddy of the salmon pool had
shown any interest in either a dry or a wet fly. Indeed, the future seemed
bleak for the fisherman despite the beauty of the day. The next pool
downstream for which I was making was a long and somewhat
uninteresting one, holding salmon when the water was high, and some
trout, but a pool with little feature and of comparatively little interest.
Still, the day was yet young and something had to be done. The intervening stretch of water beside which I was walking was broad and
rather shallow, but at one point the slope of the river bed threw the
current over towards the right bank on which I was walking. Hitherto I had paid little attention to this piece of water which certainly had
no reputation for being of any quality—if indeed it was ever fished;
but now I looked at it more closely and realised that with the bulk of
the water on my side, a strong stream some four or five feet deep and
several yards wide was flowing beside and a few feet below me as I
walked. There were no signs of trout rising, but it seemed worth
trying, and as the breeze seemed likely to be for once favourable for
an upstream cast, while trout lying in such water were almost sure to
be large ones, I made a wide detour and came back to the riverside
some fifty yards lower down. Now facing upstream I could see that
here and there were tiny bays at the edge of the strong stream caused
no doubt by pieces of turf falling down the steep bank above, and so
making little eddies and back-waters beside the main stream in which
large trout might feed. Looking upstream I could see several such
eddies where trout were in fact rising. The margin of error in casting
upstream was small, for if the fly fell too far out it would be immediately caught by the swift water, while if the error were the other

way there was a great risk of the fly becoming caught on the grass, rushes or occasional small willows growing on the bank. On this comparatively windless day the odds were not so long as they were to prove in future, and by the time I had reached the top of the 50 yard stretch I had three good trout averaging about 1½lb and all hooked in the small eddies under the bank. Each, as in the narrow pool above, when hooked made straight out into the strong stream and had to be played from far above, till such time as I could get down below them, and many an anxious moment I had; but on this day, too, the luck held and no trout were lost.

Some days later, on the same stretch of water, I was very near being the most unwilling cause of a sad tragedy. On this day, as was so often to happen, the breeze blew strongly downstream in my face. I had with difficulty made a fairly long cast upstream, gathering in the line quickly by hand as the fly floated down. On this occasion the loose line falling at my feet had got tangled and to remedy the position I pulled in nearly all the line, leaving only a few feet of line and the cast and fly dragging on the surface of the water below me. As I struggled to get the line disentangled a movement from the bank a few yards upstream caught my eye, and looking up I was fascinated to see a brood of about eight tiny ducklings emerge from the bank and set off downstream. So tight-packed were the little birds that I believe the cloth cap which I was wearing would easily have covered the lot. They passed me going downstream at a great pace. Next moment I felt a slight pull on the line dragging on the surface and saw to my horror that one small duckling had fouled my fly and was being dragged on the surface by the fast current. I had no alternative but to pull the little bird as quickly and as gently as possible up the bank, while it, poor scrap, shouted blue murder. Fortunately my fly had only caught in the down of one small wing, without penetrating the skin. Having got the tiny bird into my hand I was able to extricate the hook and lying on the bank with my arm at full stretch I dropped the duckling back on the surface of the water, when it lost no time in setting off at its best speed to rejoin its brothers and sisters, by now out of sight but probably sheltering under the bank at no great distance.

The episode of the small duckling reminded me of an incident not far from the same spot in the previous year. On this part of the Don there are certain stretches where the banks for some distance back from the river are covered with a thick growth of a plant with rough-ish broad leaves growing some six to eight inches high and with yellow pendant blossoms. Though common on this part of Donside, I have not seen it elsewhere, but almost certainly it is a member of the com-frey family. Growing usually ankle deep or more, it often occurs in thick clumps at least a foot high. Passing one day in mid-May along the bank of the river not very far from such a clump, a mallard duck got up, it seemed rather clumsily and slowly. She had all the appearance of a nesting bird and I very cautiously looked about for a nest. None was to be seen, but keeping in mind the thick clump of comfrey so near, I knelt down till my eye was nearly on ground level. From this angle I could see what appeared to be a small rabbit-run leading through the comfrey, invisible from overhead, and ending in a nesting cavity in the middle of the tall clump. The tunnel was several feet long and I did not dare to put my hand along it even with the greatest care; but enough light came through the clump to allow me to see a nest full of duck's eggs.

We came to Donside again in late July of the same year (1971). The river was still pathetically low and even such salmon as may have struggled up in the early spring, braving pollution and disease, had clearly passed on up towards the headwaters. Not one single salmon was to be seen in a week during which we covered several miles of river, and, as in most trout streams in Scotland, the trout fishing was by now far past its best. Indeed, trout fishing was almost at a stand still, except possibly in the evening, and my wife and I are now too old for evening fishing. During the five days on which we fished we caught a total of only five trout, and of those only one is worth recording. I had come to have some confidence in the deep stream under the bank near where the episode of the duckling had taken place, and tried it again and again though with slight success. Then one day despite the usual downstream wind I persevered, concentrating on a very short stretch nearly at the top of the deep water where there was an eddy close under the bank, extremely tempting but equally perilous owing to overhanging willow and other growth. Two casts fell too far out from the bank, the fly being immediately caught and whisked away by the fast stream. A third, closer in to the bank, seemed to be tempting Providence, but for once it fell well on the inner side of the rapid river and was caught by the eddy. As I watched it circle round, a brown nose appeared and the fly was sucked in. The trout was without a doubt firmly hooked, but it seemed asking too much to hope to catch what was clearly a large trout hooked within inches of a strong stream which extended for several hundred yards below me. I was wearing waders—luckily only the kind which come to the thigh —but the bank on which I stood was rough, with many holes, completely hidden by meadow-sweet and other waterside plants which came up to my waist. I was, besides, tired towards the end of a long day. The trout, repeating the tactics of so many of its colleagues on other days in other years, shot out into the strong stream and was soon far below me. Indeed, in a very short time, despite such perilous and stumbling run as I could achieve, all my line was out and much of my backing. I had had no sight of the trout and was only sure that it was very large. It seemed impossible that exhausted as I was and stumbling through waist-high meadow-sweet I could hope to retain contact with a large trout still running rapidly downstream at the end of nearly fifty yards of line ending in a cast of only 3lb breaking strain. Soon the inevitable happened and I fell headlong into an unseen ditch. Still the rod was somehow held upright and the line was still running free, though before I had stumbled to my feet the trout had gained several yards on me and the drum of the reel was almost empty. At last, however, the stream was slightly broadening out and becoming less deep though no less rapid as it approached the neck of the salmon pool below, half-way down which my wife was fishing. One difficult hurdle, however, remained to be crossed. Could I get down from the high bank into the shallowing water where I would have better— and visible—footing? A slight and fairly gentle break in the bank made this possible, and now for the first time I felt a slight hope of catching my trout. A few yards farther and the trout was through the rough water at the neck of the lower pool and into deeper, slower water where it no longer had the advantage of the current, and where for the first time since hooking it I began slowly to recover line. My wife was now in sight and in answer to my almost despairing calls she quickly reeled in her line and came up the bank as fast as possible to meet me, believing as she well might that, almost incredibly, I had hooked a salmon. Now in the deep slow water the trout fortunately proved as exhausted as I was, and in another few minutes a trout of 3½lb was in the net, close on a quarter of a mile from where it had been hooked. Though it was not the biggest brown trout I have caught in sixty-five years of fishing, the fight with it was without doubt the hardest I have ever had.

Although the fight with the big brown trout took place during our most recent visit to Donside in July, I think our most lasting memory of that lovely valley goes back to a day in the last days of May in this same year. It was a day of brilliant sunshine, without a cloud in the sky. For the first part of the day we fished carefully the salmon pool which I have described so fully above, together with the water above and below it, but hardly a trout rose, and towards midday we returned to the flat boulder to rest and review the situation. It was far too early to give up, yet further fishing seemed useless, at least till much later in the day. The brilliant weather tempted us to climb to higher ground to get a more distant view up Donside. So putting our very frugal lunch in a haversack we set off slowly up the hill above us. The slope was steeper than we had bargained for and the sun was very hot; but the widening view as we climbed drew us on. Skirting the edge of the plantation, we came to a small patch of level ground in a gap between two clumps of golden broom. Here we sat to regain our breath, to eat our lunch and to look down on the river below us and upstream to the farther hills. Rested again, we pushed on past the planted ground and so came over a slight watershed to a point where high hill pasture gave way to ground covered by the pale green foliage of young blaeberry and at last to heather. Following tracks made by the hill cattle we came, almost hidden among low bushes of whin and broom, on small clumps of mushrooms, the earliest I have ever seen, especially at an altitude of 1,200 or 1,300 feet. Cock grouse rose on either side of the track—a good sign, for it almost certainly meant that the hens were fully occupied on more domestic matters. Turning downhill again we stood for a time at the top edge of the pasture ground before beginning the steep descent. From where we stood we could trace the windings of the Don from a mile or two downstream, to the pools directly below us and then farther and farther up into the hills to the west, the windings of the river sometimes hidden by the rounded hills through which it flows, and sometimes showing themselves in silver gleams growing smaller and smaller and finally disappearing from sight as the far hills closed in.

CHAPTER 16

In praise of my trout rod

When, some two weeks ago, I took down my trout rod after a not unproductive morning's fishing on our small loch, I reflected somewhat sadly that, though now at the very end of September (1970) trout could still be legally caught, the pleasures of the trout-fishing season were virtually over for another year. As I put the rod into its case I was reminded of what I had noticed earlier in the season, that some of the tyings of the split cane required renewing, while the whole rod was in need of revarnishing. So a few days later I handed it over to Messrs Hardy Bros in Edinburgh, explaining what I wanted done. The work, I emphasised, was to be confined to the retying, where needed, and the revarnishing. I was well aware that the rubber knob on the base of the rod had been almost completely worn through on one side, while at the place where my thumb rested on the cork handle when the rod was in use, the cork after more than fifty years' wear had grown a little soft and quite appreciably hollowed out by constant pressure. These minor defects were to be allowed to remain untouched. My insistence on this arose from a very real if sentimental feeling for the past history of the rod and as this may be of some interest, it seems worth while to put part of it on record.

In the spring of 1917, after a number of years at school in Edinburgh it was decided that my schooling should be completed at Winchester, and here at the start of the summer term, or Cloister Time as it was more picturesquely called, I went. Of all public schools I would think that Winchester, steeped in tradition and ancient custom is, or certainly at that time was, one of the least suitable for a boy to make a start under somewhat unusual, and certainly unorthodox, circumstances; and in my case the circumstances were unusual. I was over sixteen years of age, nearly three years more than the usual age for entering the school, and I had up till that time not been called on to face the rough and tumble, the hardships, such as they were, and the fairly strict rules and regulations of life at a public school; but at that period during the First World War orthodox arrangements for entry to public schools, in common with so much else, had been upset, and so my entry to Winchester at an unusually advanced age became possible. My not unnatural apprehension as to what lay ahead of me was tempered to no small extent by the knowledge that I was likely to have the great good fortune while in the school to be able at times to fish one of the best stretches of the Itchen under the most favourable auspices; and it is here that the history of my trout rod begins.

When I went south to Winchester for my first term in that summer of 1917, I took with me a good but rather whippy greenheart rod of 10 feet, which I had used for some years with good effect on the burns of south Perthshire and on lochs both in Perthshire and Argyllshire. In his *Fly Fishing*, Lord Grey of Fallodon has described how the novelty and strangeness of his early days at Winchester obliterated any thought of fishing the Itchen during his first weeks at the school. My own experience during the early part of Cloister Time 1917 was very similar, a circumstance further complicated by illness during the early weeks of the term; but illness and strangeness passed as the term went on, and about the end of June a letter came from Lord Grey inviting me to go to Itchen Abbas and have a day's fishing with him on the next whole holiday, which was known in the school as Hatch Thoke. Never was invitation more gratefully and eagerly accepted. I recall vividly the excitement and anticipation with which I bicycled the 4 miles from Winchester to Itchen Abbas keeping a careful look-out for the grass-grown avenue leading between old lime trees to his cottage, of which Lord Grey's letter had told me, and taking with me the faithful, but as it transpired the very inadequate greenheart rod which had done such useful service in Scotland. Of that first day's fishing with Lord Grey I have only a general recollection. I know that I caught a trout and I know too that the wide knowledge and infinite kindness of my host combined with my first full realisation of the beauty of Hampshire water-meadows to make the day a supremely happy one. The weaknesses of my whippy greenheart rod as an instrument for throwing a dry fly with delicacy and accuracy were on that first day painfully apparent. I learned later that Lord Grey had reported in the proper quarter that I was a keen, and even perhaps potentially an efficient, dry fly fisherman sadly handicapped by inferior equipment, and at Christmas in that same year my uncle presented me with a new rod specially chosen for me by Lord Grey for use on the Itchen. The new rod, modelled on one which Messrs Hardy Bros had earlier built for Lord Grey himself, was a two-piece split cane rod, $9\frac{1}{2}$ feet in length, strong and fairly stiff in action as a dry fly rod should be, and known as the 'Knockabout'.

There was little opportunity to test the rod in action before the coming summer, but during the summer term of 1918 I fished at Itchen Abbas on each of the whole holidays, usually in the company of my cousin, who was in the same house at Winchester. Occasionally Lord Grey himself was at the cottage, but often he was kept in London by his work at the Foreign Office, and when this happened we always found that he had instructed his house-keeper to give us lunch and an evening meal at such hour as we wanted it. These for me were days of intense happiness, ending almost invariably in a hurried bicycle ride back to Winchester only just in time for Names-calling. Indeed, on one occasion when the rise of trout had been unusually good and prolonged we arrived back too late and found that the house roll had already been sent in to our Housemaster with our names marked as 'Absent'. Greatly daring, I stole into the Housemaster's study in the hope of amending the roll before he saw it. To my consternation he entered the study by one door as I came in by the other, a confrontation which threatened extreme embarrassment on my side. But fortunately our Housemaster was a keen if not a very knowledgeable angler. He knew that we had been at Itchen Abbas for the day and guessed that the evening rise had caused our fall from grace. So the crisis was surmounted by frankness on our side and understanding on his, an outcome made all the easier by the fact that our catch of eight trout averaging fully 1½lb each went far to feed the Housemaster and at least most of the members of the House on the following day.

Those who know Lord Grey's *Fly fishing*—and surely no finer book on fly fishing exists in the English language—will recall how painfully but rapidly his education in dry fly fishing progressed, from 1 fish caught in his first summer at Winchester to 13 in his second, 32 in his third and 76 in his fourth. I can claim no rapid increase in skill in any way comparable to the achievements of one who came to be widely recognised as a complete master of his craft; but at least, armed with the new rod, I learned to throw a dry fly with some accuracy and I see from the fishing diary which I kept at that time that in four day's fishing at Itchen Abbas during the summer term of 1919 the total catch was 35 trout, of which the largest weighed 1lb 14oz, 2lb and 2lb 5oz. Before I left Winchester at the end of that summer term the Itchen and its trout had ceased to fill me with feelings of complete inadequacy, while the beauty of chalk stream water flowing through Hampshire water-meadows in summer had brought to me a happiness which both in realisation and in retrospect has never left me.

To attempt to write in any detail the history of my Knockabout rod since the day I first used it on the Itchen in 1918 would lead me into many paths of angling reminiscences and autobiographical detail which it is not my present purpose to pursue; but some incidents, chosen almost at random, may indicate the many different types of water on which I have used this rod, the strains and stresses to which from time to time it has been exposed, and the extent to which, over more than half a century, it has entwined itself around my heart till I have come to think of it as almost part of myself.

Four years at Oxford followed my Winchester days and here in the summer terms there were occasional visits to Fairford and Bibury on the Gloucestershire Coln, and at least one further visit to Itchen Abbas, in all of which my Knockabout accompanied me. At home in Perthshire I had long fought a losing battle on our local river the Earn with quite large trout which showed little interest in the wet flies which I offered them. Now with dry flies and a dry fly rod in my fishing armoury the odds were less uneven, and on many an evening in June and July I fought long and not always fruitless battles against large trout rising in the growing dusk.

Soon after my return from Oxford to a legal apprenticeship in Edinburgh, my brother and I started in our now restricted holidays, to make fishing expeditions farther afield, and from this period dates my discovery of the wide possibilities of Aberdeenshire and Banffshire not only for the salmon fisherman but for the dry fly angler. One of our first visits was to a part of the River Deveron a few miles upstream from Banff. Here, as early as mid-April big hatches of fly would appear and the dry fly came into its own. Here, too, my Knockabout got its first experience of really rough usage. A good trout had risen in midstream a little way above me, but within reasonable casting distance. My fly came over it and instead of the expected and hoped for rise of a trout, a great head and shoulders emerged and the floating fly was engulfed. The ensuing fight was long and stubborn, and when some twenty minutes later a well-mended kelt of some 12lb was netted it was with some pride and relief that I found my rod as straight and unharmed as ever. Years later, another part of the Deveron farther upstream became familiar to me. Here too, the hatch of fly occasionally rivalled what I have sometimes seen in Hampshire, and the trout fed greedily. On this part of the river my difficulties arose not only from adverse winds and the many other ills which afflict the dry fly fisherman, but from human idiosyncracies as well. My host was a keen and single-minded salmon fisherman caring much for the salmon records of his piece of river, but little for trout. So it came that I would set off in the mornings carrying my salmon rod ready for action and much in evidence and taking my Knockabout unobtrusively in its canvas case. On many a day after the salmon rod had been used—often in vain—for long enough to satisfy my conscience, a sudden rise of good trout led to the hurried putting together of the trout rod, with cast and dry fly. Many a pleasant and fruitful hour was thus spent, the pleasure only very slightly spoiled by the knowledge of my host's disapproval. The last day on which I fished that stretch of the Deveron the trout rose exceptionally well and my catch included one of 3lb.

For four years in the 1930s my brother and I rented for a few weeks in August and September a small river on the west coast of Skye with a large extent of grouse shooting. The quality of the shooting was not high, but quite a number of good coveys were to be found if one had a pointer and were prepared, as we were, for long walks. The river held mainly sea-trout and was wholly a spate river; but a few salmon came up it in times of flood and it was here that my Knockabout and I were involved in a prolonged fight with a salmon of well over 10lb which was foul-hooked in the dorsal fin. With such an adversary and such a rod, the odds were grossly unfair, and when after nearly three hours the fish was lost in growing darkness I felt real relief that my arm could now be rested and that, once again, my little rod had emerged from the struggle unharmed.

One fault, and one fault only, had I to find with my lovely rod. A two-piece rod is admirable in strength and action, and mine could be used with equal ease and pleasure for wet or dry fly. Where possible I tend to use the dry fly, as giving me more pleasure in the rising and hooking of trout, and bringing to the fly, as I believe, the bigger and more active fish; but for journeys by car or train a two-piece rod is awkward and dangerous even when the dismantled rod in its case measures under 5 feet. For years I partially solved the problem, by tying the dismantled rod in its case to a thin piece of wood, but this was not very satisfactory and it was only after my wife presented me with an aluminium case that long journeys with my rod could be undertaken with safety.

So the years passed and my little rod and I widened our knowledge and experience of trout streams both at home and abroad. For many years no chance of fishing again on Hampshire chalk streams came my way, but more recently it has been my good fortune to fish with a friend once each year on the upper Test. Here, above Whitchurch, the Test is a smaller river than the Itchen at Itchen Abbas. The water is almost everywhere shallower, while its clearness makes even the most cautious approach to a trout, let alone casting a fly over it, a matter of the greatest difficulty. But the lessons learned at Winchester and on other dry fly waters since then proved not unprofitable, and here on the Test only a mile or two from its source trout were caught and memories of Winchester days were most happily renewed.

And now that I have recalled in this and the earlier chapters of this book some of the scenes of beauty and of happiness in nearly all of which my little rod and I have shared, I know that only a small part has been told; but perhaps what has been written is enough to explain why in handing my rod to Hardy's last week I was insistent that only really neccessary repairs should be done. For the rest the rod will remain as it is and has been for so very many years, to continue, I hope, to give me pleasure for such fishing days as may be still to come. At least I feel sure that had Lord Grey, in choosing the rod for me in the autumn of 1917, been able to foresee the long years of happiness which it was to give, he would indeed have been well pleased.